Smol00636

J6C
(And)

Studying Your Own School

0803961146

Studying Your Own School

An Educator's Guide to Qualitative Practitioner Research

Gary L. Anderson, Kathryn Herr, Ann Sigrid Nihlen

CORWIN PRESS, INC.
A Sage Publications Company
Thousand Oaks, California

For information address:

 Corwin Press, Inc.
2455 Teller Road
Thousand Oaks, California 91320

SAGE Publications Ltd.
6 Bonhill Street
London EC2A 4PU
United Kingdom

SAGE Publications India Pvt. Ltd.
M-32 Market
Greater Kailash I
New Delhi 110 048 India

Printed in the United States of America

Library of Congress Cataloging-in-Publication Data

Main entry under title:

Anderson, Gary L., 1948-
Studying your own school: an educator's guide to qualitative practitioner research / authors, Gary L. Anderson, Kathryn Herr, Ann Sigrid Nihlen.
p. cm.
Includes bibliographical references and index.
ISBN 8039-6113-8 (alk. paper). — ISBN 0-8039-6114-6 (pbk. alk. paper).
1. Action research in education. 2. Education—Research
I. Herr, Kathryn. II. Nihlen, Ann Sigrid. III. Title.
LB1028.24.A53 1994
370'.783—dc20   94-30532

This book is printed on acid-free paper that meets Environmental Protection Agency standards for recycled paper.

98 10 9 8 7 6

Corwin Press Production Editor: Diane S. Foster

Contents

Foreword   ix
    by *Susan E. Noffke*

Acknowledgments   xiii

Preface   xv

About the Authors   xxiii

1. What Is Practitioner Research?   1
   Defining Practitioner Research   2
   Working Assumptions   4
   Conclusion   7

2. Merging Educational Practice and Research:
   A New Paradigm   9

   Practitioner Research: History   9
   The Multiple Traditions of Practitioner Research   9

Beginnings of Practitioner Research 10
The Action Research Tradition 11
Action Research in Education 13
The Teacher-as-Researcher Movement in Great Britain 14
Participatory Research: The Legacy of Freire 16
Action Science 18
The Teacher Researcher Movement in North America 19
Practitioner Research: From Academic
    Tradition to Social Movement 23

Practitioner Research: Epistemology 27
Is Practitioner Research a "Valid" Way of Knowing? 27
Criteria for "Validity" in Practitioner Research 29
Are the Findings of Practitioner Research Generalizable? 33

Practitioner Research: Politics 36
The Politics of Knowledge, Institutional Change,
    and Professionalism 36
What Is "Politics?" 36
Institutional Micropolitics 37
The Politics of Redefining Professionalism 40
The Politics of Educational Knowledge 42
The Politics of Schooling as a Social Institution 44
Conclusion 44

3. What Does Practitioner Research Look Like? 46
Research in the Classroom:
    Monica Richards and the "Bums" of 8H 49
Developing Teacher Voice: Robyn Russell 55
Students as Coinvestigators in
    the Research Process: Suzanne SooHoo 61
Expanding Theory Through Teacher Research:
    Cindy Ballenger 66
Group Process in Support of Practitioner Research:
    The Principals' Group 70
A Research Seminar for Teachers:
    The Educators' Forum 77
Final Thoughts 79

4. Empowerment and Practitioner Research:
An Example 80
Getting Started 80

The Process of Empowerment 83
Is This Racism? 85
Responding to Their World 88
Political and Methodological Implications
    of Empowerment 95
The Negotiation of Multiple Roles and
    Multiple Levels of Reality 96
Transformation Becomes a Kind of War 100
Epilogue 101
Discussion 102
But Is It Research? 103

5. Qualitative Research Approaches for
  Everyday Realities 106
Assumptive Modes 108
The Research Question 114

Methods 115
Interviews 115
Observation 129
Archives and Documents 151
Journals and Diaries 153

Analysis 155
Ongoing Analysis and Reflection 155
The Final Analysis 156

Multiple Methods Studies 168
Educational Ethnography 168
Oral History 169
Case Studies 170

6. Toward a New Paradigm 171
Methodological Adaptations: Practitioners
    Looking for Appropriate Techniques 176
Methods That Surface Tacit Knowledge 178
Working in a Community of Inquiry:
    Buffering the Isolation 181
Conclusion 181

References 183

Index 199

Foreword

Over the past decade there has been a quiet, yet substantive change in the role of practitioners in educational research. Grassroots efforts in action research and other forms of practitioner research have highlighted the importance of educators' own understanding of their practice. Within the research and teacher education institutions, and most recently from within the state have come endorsements, exhortations and reward structures claiming the benefits of researching one's own practice. Increasing attention from many levels has been paid to self (individual and collective) study as a means for both teacher development and educational reform, often including attention to the need for greater social justice in and through education. Yet there has also been, despite this remarkable growth in projects involving educational practitioners in various aspects of research, remarkable confusion, especially in the United States, over the meaning of terms such as *action research* and *practitioner research*.

In this context, *Studying Your Own School* makes an important contribution. Without assuming a parochial stance, the work highlights important and complex historical, epistemological, and methodological questions in an accessible style.

It is ironic that all too often the literature on practitioner research reproduces the same separation between theory and practice that it seeks to subvert. Those writing about it do so within the language and publication systems of universities. As such, there is a separation between abstract works about practitioner research and "practical" guides. In the latter, there is a tendency to reduce its complexities to the level of a short "How to do it" manual pared of the core of personal, ethical, and political dimensions that are central to practitioner research. In this book, however, there is a balance between thorough access to the vast international academic literature, strong narrative text that allows readers to "feel" how research proceeds, and a good introduction to issues of data collection and analysis. Questions of paradigmatic status, validity, and the politics of knowledge production are addressed alongside examples of the lived experience of doing research. Methods of engaging in research are usefully summarized, but within a framework reminding us that the techniques for practitioner research are not merely a parroting of those of traditional social science but rather are emerging in response to educational lives and concerns.

Studying Your Own School can assist teachers and other educators, collaboratively as well as individually, in using research to improve both the quality and the justice of education in all of our own schools. This is an era in which the danger in practitioner research is clearly the same as that in other contemporary reforms, such as shared decision making and school-based management. The problems in education are not confined to school buildings. The larger political and economic context of schooling is one in which poverty and racism are central dynamics. For many works on practitioner research, the process has been reduced to a few short steps, individually taken, to improve the technical efficiency of one's practice. In actual practice, practitioner research is much more. It can offer a collaborative means to richer understandings of education and to the identification of what I refer to as the "spaces for ethically defensible, politically strategic action" (Noffke, forthcoming). In decision making, in management, and in research there must be a focus on understanding technical, social, and political aspects of issues as they emerge in action. *Studying Your Own School* builds on the experiences of practitioners, potentially enhancing both understanding and action.

Susan E. Noffke

Acknowledgments

We would like to thank the site-based research class at the University of New Mexico and the following individuals for their valuable input: Susan Noffke, Mary Beth Poole, Michelle Raisch, Ernie Stringer, Christine Jakicic, Patricia Irvine, and Don Zancanella.

*   *   *

I owe a considerable debt to the teachers, principals, and school leadership teams of Emerson Elementary School. They have always welcomed me, allowed me free access to whatever they were doing and planning, and allowed me to wander their halls. When they asked me to teach a course for them on site, we began a journey that includes, but does not end, with this book. As teacher researchers, they shared their perspectives and hopes for developing practitioner research. For this, I thank them.

STUDYING YOUR OWN SCHOOL

I also want to thank the many students who have taken my qualitative research courses over the years; I have learned a great deal from their questions as well as from their research.

Ann Sigrid Nihlen

*   *   *

We would like to thank Owen Creightney, "the boys' group," Laurie Hause, Deborah Klien, Vivianne Robinson, Grace Brown, and the Philadelphia "principals' group": Arlene Holtz, Jolly Christman, Holly Perry, Joanruth Hirshman, Rita Spelkoman, and Mollie Williams.

Kathryn Herr and Gary L. Anderson

Preface

For me, it [teacher research] was part of learning how to be a learner again and thinking about what made that exciting for me. Then, when you get back into that mode, you think, how can I create that for my students? . . . I enjoy what I'm doing again, I'm not just making it through the day anymore.

Stephanie Mansdoerfer, teacher,
La Cueva High School, Albuquerque, NM

The above testimony by a high school teacher captures the kind of excitement we have encountered regarding practitioner research, both within the academic research community and within the public school system. Practitioners are excited because such research can lead to professional renewal and improvement of practice. Academics are excited because practitioner research represents, among other things, a more grounded approach to the creation of new knowledge about educational practices.

We have attempted to create a book that is the result of a dialogue between the experience-based insights from the world of practice and the methodological and theoretical insights of the academic community. Although representing different professional cultures, those who work in colleges of education and those who work in schools are beginning to recognize that they each have a different kind of knowledge—each with its own criteria of validity—to share. School practitioners are beginning to demystify the hierarchical nature of the so-called expert knowledge of academics, and academics are beginning to realize that the old model of knowledge creation (in universities), dissemination (through academic journals), and utilization (by practitioners) is not working.

A growing number of teachers, counselors, and administrators are collaborating with universities in a variety of capacities. Colleges of education are increasingly demanding that their faculty have extensive and recent practitioner experience, and that faculty spend greater amounts of time in schools. Although ivory tower college of education professors who have not set foot in a school in 20 years can still be found, they are nearing retirement.

This book is a school-university collaboration. We represent a variety of backgrounds. Gary L. Anderson has worked for 13 years as a teacher and school administrator and is currently a faculty member in the College of Education at the University of New Mexico. Kathryn Herr is a teacher/counselor engaged in research in a middle school. During the 1993-94 academic year she took a one-year leave to work as a visiting professor at the University of New Mexico, where she taught practitioner research and worked with local professional development schools. Ann Sigrid Nihlen, also a faculty member at the University of New Mexico, is an educational anthropologist who has spent much of her professional career observing classrooms through the eyes of an ethnographer. In recent years, she worked closely with professional development schools on collaborative teacher research projects. We bring a variety of experiences to this endeavor, and these experiences, we hope, provide a series of checks and balances between insider and outsider perspectives.

In this book we try to maintain a broad definition of what constitutes "research" and an open mind to the various perspectives of practitioner research. At one point, we considered replacing the term "research" with "inquiry"; we decided, however, that although much practitioner research might stretch the conventional notion of research, we did not want to create the impression that academics do research and practitioners merely do "inquiry." We like the tension of stretching what "counts" as research, and seeing the dissonance that academics might feel as healthy.

Even though we have been school practitioners, it has been a struggle for the two university-based authors to understand that insider, action-oriented research is a new paradigm incompatible in many ways with the epistemology of the social sciences, regardless of how qualitative the approach. Having an active and empowered practitioner researcher as coauthor provided a check on our paradigmatic ethnocentrism.

Disciplinary blinders also had to be dealt with. Don Zancanella, a colleague from English education, politely but firmly reminded us that "many composition and English teachers see at least part of their professional identity and allegiance as being not in a scientific or social science community, but in the arts/humanities community where narrative knowledge is highly valued." Because English teachers and teachers of writing are in the vanguard of the teacher research movement, this helps explain why practitioner research does not merely look like an "insider" version of social science. Many university faculty who teach courses in practitioner research have not dealt with these issues, and see their role as turning practitioners into quasi-ethnographers.

We have tried to write both a practical and a scholarly book, as well as to provide a resource that practitioners can use to access other work in this area. We know of no other book on practitioner research that provides as thorough a bibliography of extant work about and by practitioner researchers.

We also have tried to keep in mind the fact that practitioners do research for many reasons. Some do dissertations at their own sites. Some study their own settings to improve their practice. Some see themselves as producers of knowledge that other practitioners, as well as academics, might find useful. Some see themselves as part of a grassroots movement to challenge older paradigms of educational practice. Some critique the schooling practices that help reproduce social inequalities in the wider society. Although we are biased toward viewing practitioner researchers as critical change agents within their schools, we have tried to write a book that will speak to each of the above-mentioned purposes.

Description of Contents

In Chapter 1, we provide the reader with a loose definition of practitioner research. The purpose of providing a definition is not to fix parameters, but to give the reader who may be encountering practitioner research for the first time some general categories with which to approach subsequent chapters. We also lay out a series of assumptions about teacher research. These are themes that serve as a subtext for the rest of the book.

Educational practitioners have been doing some form of systematic inquiry for as long as there have been schools. However, the notion of inquiring practitioners has been written about and studied only relatively recently. In the first section of Chapter 2, we provide a review of the various ways that practitioner research has manifested itself in different times and social contexts. It is a paradigm of research that has surfaced at different times and in different places over the past 100 years. We feel it is important that the beginning practitioner researcher be aware that he or she is engaging in work that has a long, important, and controversial history.

In the second and third sections of Chapter 2 we provide the reader with a sense of the epistemological and political issues associated with practitioner research. We agree with Cochran-Smith and Lytle (1993) that practitioner research represents a potential new knowledge base in education, and that we must begin to discuss how this new knowledge, which emerges from action and from inside schools, is created and shared.

We also discuss the ways that insider research is political. By political we mean not only the ways that practitioner research can be viewed as a threat within institutional and district politics, but also the "politics of knowledge," in which school practitioners struggle to legitimate the currently devalued knowledge base that exists in schools.

In Chapter 3, we try to capture the diversity of current approaches to practitioner research by summarizing a variety of practitioner research studies. Throughout the book we cite numerous other studies that the reader can access. We believe that the best thing aspiring practitioner researchers can do is to read other practitioners' studies. For the first time since action research appeared many decades ago, there is a critical mass of published studies and conference papers that report practitioner research in education. Readers may be surprised to find that most practitioner studies are not like the neat and tidy qualitative research studies published in educational journals. In fact, as the reader will discover, many of the studies exist only as conference papers and fugitive documents, difficult to access. This is changing, as new journals dedicated to practitioner research are in the planning stages.

Whereas qualitative researchers are mainly concerned with disseminating their findings about the research setting to a scientific community, practitioner researchers are most concerned with recording change processes based on actions they have taken in their settings. We feel there is an immediacy and a healthy disregard for convention in practitioner research that most qualitative research lacks.

In Chapter 4, we attempt to bring previous themes together through a process-oriented narrative of a 3-year practitioner research study undertaken by coauthor Herr. Unlike Chapter 3, which concentrates on the findings of the studies, this chapter focuses on the research process, with an eye to opening a window onto the decision making of a practitioner researcher as Herr encounters the ever-changing, action-oriented, and political nature of the setting in which she is both practitioner and researcher. Herr describes the ways that goals of empowerment and the defensive mechanisms of institutions create an environment in which the practitioner researcher must tread with care. This chapter also graphically illustrates what we reiterate several times throughout the book—that practitioner research is not neat and tidy.

In teaching courses on practitioner research, we have found that practitioners have made important modifications to traditional qualitative research methods. In Chapter 5, we provide the reader with a user-friendly guide to qualitative methods, while at the same time indicating how practitioners are modifying these methods to meet the constraints and opportunities they encounter in their schools.

Finally, in Chapter 6, we discuss some ways that practitioner researchers are pushing the edges of what currently "counts" as research.

Toward a New Paradigm of Social Inquiry

> The conventional weapons of research are cumbersome;
> heavy field pieces dragged slowly into position—hardly suit-
> able for the swift-moving, rapidly changing targets of an
> action programme. (Smith, 1975, p. 194)

For too long researchers in colleges of education have felt like
second-class citizens with regard to their university colleagues in
the arts and sciences. They have sensed that their research in action-
oriented settings and their split commitment between the scientific
community and practitioner community made their research not so
much inferior as fundamentally different.

Practitioners, who could be characterized as third-class citizens
in this academic pecking order, feel the same tensions with regard
to educational researchers. Most graduate courses in research are
designed to teach practitioners how to consume research done by
academic researchers. Seldom is it even suggested that practitioners
could do research themselves, unless they were to enroll in a university doctoral program.

Books have been written by academic researchers in the last 20
years about the differences between positivistic and naturalistic
(qualitative) paradigms. Only recently have most educational researchers made their peace—at least in public—with the legitimacy
of both. Now academics are watching the emergence of a third way
of knowing education—research done by educational practitioners.
Although it bears some resemblance to the naturalistic paradigm, it
differs in several important ways.

1. Knowledge is not produced for a scientific community, but
   rather for an interpretive community, consisting primarily—
   though not exclusively—of school practitioners.
2. Unlike naturalistic research, which involves the observation,
   description, and interpretation of educational settings, practitioner research aims primarily at the transformation of these
   settings.

3. Unlike naturalistic research, practitioner research is done within an action-oriented setting in which reflection on action is the driving force of the research. This tension inherent in combining action and research is captured in the term traditionally used to describe this type of inquiry: "action research."

We believe it is time for educators—both academics and practitioners—to stop apologizing for our research and clinging to paradigms that do not fit our reality. In addition to Smith (1975), Lindblom and Cohen (1979) and others long ago called into question the usefulness of most social-science research, which approaches social change through top-down, inside-out models of "social engineering." Modernist paradigms in the arts and sciences are falling like dominos. When the smoke clears, social scientists may understand that while they have been defending their modernist canon, educators—researchers and practitioners—have collaboratively been exploring a new paradigm of research with the potential to bring about social change from the bottom-up and the inside-out. We hope this book moves us closer to that goal.

About the Authors

Gary L. Anderson is a former teacher and principal who is currently an Associate Professor in the College of Education at the University of New Mexico. He has written articles on qualitative research methodology and studies of the principalship, including "Critical Ethnography in Education: Origins, Current Status, and New Directions" in *Review of Educational Research* and "Toward a Critical Constructivist Approach to School Administration: Invisibility, Legitimation, and the Study of Non-events" in *Educational Administration Quarterly*. His other books include *The Micropolitics of Educational Leadership: From Control to Empowerment* (with Joseph Blase), and *Educational Qualitative Research in Latin America: The Struggle for a New Paradigm* (with Martha Montero-Sieburth).

Kathryn Herr has been actively engaged in practitioner research as a middle school counselor and teacher for over 4 years. She has studied issues of ethnic identity and gender relations in early adolescence at her work site. The results of her work have been published in the *International Journal of Qualitative Studies in Education* and *The 1992 Politics of Education Association Yearbook*. She is currently a Visiting Professor in the College of Education at the University of New Mexico and Editor of the Sage journal *Youth and Society*.

Ann Sigrid Nihlen is an Associate Professor in the Language, Literacy, and Cultural Studies Program at the College of Education at the University of New Mexico. She has taught at State University of New York at Buffalo and she was the Coordinator of Women Studies at the University of New Mexico. Currently she teaches courses on qualitative and practitioner research, anthropology and education, perspectives on sex and gender, and social class and education. She has published in the areas of gender, practitioner research, and women's studies, and sits on the editorial boards of *Frontiers: A Journal of Women* and *Youth and Society*. Her current investigations include work with the Emerson Elementary School Oral History Project, where she is a coresearcher with several teachers. She recently completed an interview study of homeless men and women, and she is also preparing a manuscript on an ethnography of white, working-class, first-grade girls.

To Lisa, Lucas, and Maya

1

What Is Practitioner Research?

Several terms in current use describe research done on site by school practitioners. The most common ones are "action research," "teacher research," "practitioner research," "site-based research," "action science," "collaborative action research," "participatory action research," "educative research," and "emancipatory praxis." As we make clear in Chapter 2, each of these terms connotes a different emphasis; in many cases, each represents different research traditions that grew out of very different social contexts.

We use the term *practitioner research* for pragmatic and philosophical reasons. Although the term *action research* is still widely used in education, it is associated in the minds of many with a particular academic social science tradition initiated by Lewin (1946). The term *teacher research* has been appropriated by a movement of teacher researchers in North America that recently has broadened to embrace all school practitioners. *Practitioner research*, a term increasingly used by school practitioners, places practitioners at the center of the enterprise.

The term practitioner research does, however, exclude other important stakeholders, such as students, parents, and other community members. It also excludes the important component of "action," which is the essence of much practitioner research. Unfortunately, the field is already cluttered with new and confusing terms. Therefore, rather than coin a new term that would be more inclusive (and considerably more cumbersome), we chose what appears to be the emerging term of choice in North America: practitioner research.

Although the plethora of terms to describe this research also reflects wide disagreement on many key issues, we provide a working definition of practitioner research, as well as a few of our working assumptions, that are used throughout the book. Practitioner research is a living, growing movement that is in the process of evolving; it is this evolution that we describe in subsequent chapters.

Defining Practitioner Research

In attempting to provide a working definition of practitioner research, we want to make it clear that every point in the following definition is hotly debated in the burgeoning literature on practitioner research. Thus, we attempt to provide a "snapshot" of how the definition is taking shape.

In basic terms, practitioner research is "insider" research done by practitioners (in this book, those working in educational settings) using their own site (classroom, institution, school district, community) as the focus of their study. It is a reflective process, but is different from isolated, spontaneous reflection in that it is deliberately and systematically undertaken, and generally requires that some form of evidence be presented to support assertions. What constitutes "evidence" or, in more traditional terms, "data," is still being debated.

Most practitioner research is oriented to some action or cycle of actions that practitioners wish to take to address a particular situation. For this reason, the term action research has traditionally been used for this type of research.

Some, including the authors, argue that practitioner research is best done in collaboration with others who have a stake in the problem under investigation, such as other educational practitioners in the setting, students, parents, or other members of the community. Sometimes collaboration involves outsiders (e.g., university faculty, consultants) who have relevant skills or resources.

Like all forms of inquiry, practitioner research is value laden. Although most practitioners hope that practitioner research will improve their practice, what constitutes "improvement" is not self-evident. It is particularly problematic in a field such as education, where there is no consensus on basic educational aims. Practitioner research takes place in educational settings that reflect a society characterized by conflicting values and an unequal distribution of resources and power.

More concise definitions exist in the growing body of literature on practitioner research. For example, McKernan (1988) describes practitioner research as "a form of self-reflective problem solving which enables practitioners to better understand and solve pressing problems in social settings" (p. 6).

McCutcheon and Jung (1990) provide the following definition: "Systematic inquiry that is collective, collaborative, self-reflective, critical, and undertaken by the participants of the inquiry. The goals of such research are the understanding of practice and the articulation of a rationale or philosophy of practice in order to improve practice" (p. 148).

Kemmis and McTaggart (1982) provide a more radical definition:

> a form of *collective,* self-reflective enquiry undertaken by participants in social situations in order to improve the rationality and justice of their own social or educational practices, as well as their understanding of these practices and the situations in which these practices are carried out. Groups of participants can be teachers, students, principals, parents, and other community members—any group with a shared concern. The approach is only action research when it is *collaborative,* though it is important to realize that the action research of the group is achieved through the *critically examined action* of the individual group members. (p. 6)

We prefer to remain as eclectic as possible with regard to a definition; however, we would like to lay out a few assumptions that form the foundation for this book.

Working Assumptions

Following are a few assumptions that we share about practitioner research. We feel that these assumptions are also widely shared within the practitioner research community.

Practitioner Research
Differs From Academic Research

Although practitioner research can borrow appropriate methods from academic research, it is fundamentally different from academic research in that it represents insider or local knowledge about a setting. There is no way an outsider, even an ethnographer who spends years as an observer, can acquire the tacit knowledge of a setting that those who must act within it daily possess. This creates obvious advantages for the practitioner researcher, but it also makes it harder for the practitioner researcher to "step back" and take a dispassionate look at the setting. This subjectivity is one of the reasons that some recommend that practitioners do research in collaboration with outsiders or with a "critical friend." This critical friend may be another insider, but one who plays a devil's advocate role. The implications of the differences between insider and outsider research are only beginning to be discussed; we review these epistemological (how we acquire and share knowledge) issues in more detail in Chapters 2 and 5.

Practitioner Research Is Political

As mentioned in our definition, we believe that no research is neutral; therefore, researchers should not be naive about how their research will be received within their setting. Although practitioner researchers need techniques for gathering and analyzing data, they also need an understanding of the ways in which practitioner research often threatens the vested interests and ideological commitments of some groups and individuals. Chapter 2 addresses the "politics" of doing practitioner research.

In Chapter 2, we attempt to discuss epistemological and political issues in a straightforward and clear manner. Many books that deal with these issues, although excellent accounts that are valuable resources for academics, tend to turn practitioners off because their discourse is pitched at academics rather than practitioners (e.g., Carr & Kemmis, 1983; Kincheloe, 1991; Winter, 1987). We want language to serve as an aid rather than an obstacle to understanding for practitioners.

On the other hand, we are disturbed by a growing anti-intellectualism on the part of some, who assume that educational practitioners only want a nuts and bolts, "what-I-can-do-on-Monday" recipe for answering "safe" and narrow questions limited to the four walls of a classroom or school. We find this trend toward "deskilling" insulting to educational practitioners, who, in our experience, desire a better understanding of their practice and its social effects. We are also beginning to understand, thanks to Argyris and Schon (1974), that there is no such thing as practice that is nontheoretical. Many of the recipes and tips for teachers that appear in practitioner journals are dripping with theoretical and ideological assumptions of which even their authors may be unaware. Part of the task of practitioner research is to strip away the unexamined theoretical baggage that has accumulated around almost everything we do in schools. To do this, we must make the familiar seem strange, the very task of much qualitative research.

There Are Many Valid Ways to Do Practitioner Research

Many practitioners are "blocked" from doing research because they have a particular image of research, acquired from a research course they took during their undergraduate or graduate studies. In all likelihood, this course taught students to do quantitative, statistical research in which representative samples, significance levels, and confounding variables were the order of the day. It is only in recent years that introductory courses present students with a fuller range of research traditions. It is hard for most practitioners to imagine doing quantitative, statistical research in their own settings. Although much research in education is of this kind, it represents only one of many options available to practitioner researchers. Some questions may be best pursued with statistical research and there are books available that address this kind of practitioner research (e.g., Brause &

Mayher, 1991; Myers, 1985; Rowntree, 1981). However, the emphasis in this book is on qualitative methodologies, which tend to be appropriated from anthropology, sociology, history, linguistics, and the humanities.

By qualitative research, we mean anything from ethnographic methods to journals and essays. We have no interest in policing what "counts" as research and what does not. Our sense is that practitioners themselves are beginning to develop criteria for distinguishing rigor from sloppiness in practitioner research. In Chapter 2, we discuss in more detail how practitioner research challenges traditional criteria for the validity of research studies.

Practitioner Research Can Empower
and Include a Greater Number of Voices

Practitioner research has the potential for empowerment and the inclusion of a greater diversity of voices in educational policy and social change. We see practitioner research as an opportunity to make the voices of those who work closest to the classroom heard. This includes not only those practitioners who work at school sites, but also the students who study there and the people who live in the school's community.

We see practitioner research not merely as individual practitioners trying to improve their practice, but as part of a larger social movement that challenges dominant research and development approaches that emphasize an outside-in, top-down approach to educational change. In other words, we believe that empowerment begins with a group of educational practitioners who view themselves not merely as consumers of someone else's knowledge, but as knowledge creators in their own right. Unless educational practitioners who are committed to empowering themselves and their students begin to take over school reform movements, practitioner research will be co-opted by those very movements, which are led by special interests more concerned with "national competitiveness" than with the welfare of children.

Although these goals are not inherently incompatible, too many children are currently viewed as socially expendable from a purely economic perspective. We personally know and work with many practitioners with a commitment to social justice working at school sites. These practitioners, through their research, are beginning to challenge the mythologies and institutional and social arrangements that lead to school failure for a disproportionate number of poor and minority students.

Practitioner Research Is Best Done Collaboratively

We believe that practitioner research is best done as part of a collaborative effort. Ideally, collaboration is done with others who have a stake in the problem under study; however, it may also be done with a group of other practitioners who are also engaged in research. These other practitioners may or may not work at the same site, but they provide the practitioner researcher with an emotional support group, a group of critical friends who can critique one's work within a context of support.

Although we do not wish to discourage isolated practitioners— many of whom may have limited access to other practitioner researchers—from engaging in research, the many advantages of collaboration are becoming increasingly apparent. In fact, many practitioner research projects have emerged unexpectedly from teacher study and support groups (Saavedra, 1994; Short, Connor, Crawford, Kahn, Kaser, & Sherman, 1993).

Conclusion

These are exciting times for practitioner research. It has the potential to bring to light important theories about practice that have been too long discredited as informal theory or "teacher lore." It can empower school practitioners by helping them discover their voices and resist attempts at deskilling. It can build collegiality and a common community of learning among practitioners, which in turn provides a model of inquiry for students. On the other hand, it can also become one more teacher in-service scheme that can be packaged and taken on the road; another implementation strategy cooked up by management to "build ownership" in schools for the latest centrally mandated reform. It can become just one more expectation—one more thing teachers are expected to do.

However, practitioners are beginning to build their own research networks. When they invite so-called experts to participate, it is increasingly on their own terms. It remains to be seen whether this movement will lead to empowerment or be co-opted as the latest teacher in-service scheme by a top-down reform movement.

2

Merging Educational Practice
and Research
A New Paradigm

Practitioner Research: History

The Multiple Traditions of Practitioner Research

Education tends to be an ahistorical field. We tend to value the new and trendy, and often fail to realize that the new is sometimes the old dressed up in new language. Practitioner research has a long and varied tradition. It is important that both practitioners and academics understand that there is a diverse intellectual tradition of practitioner research, and that this tradition is distinct from the academic research tradition in education.

Our purpose in describing the various practitioner research traditions is to illustrate that practitioner research is not new and it is not monolithic. There are differing viewpoints among these traditions about why and how practitioner research should be undertaken.

The notion of traditions is also important because what counts as valid research is what sociologists call a "social construction" (Berger & Luckmann, 1967). At different times in different social contexts, what constitutes valid ways of creating knowledge will vary. It is not by accident, for example, that emancipatory, grassroots approaches to research emerged from the oppressive social conditions of the third world. It is also not surprising from a historical perspective that positivistic, quantitative methods emerged as dominant in the field of education in the United States during the mid-20th century.

In this section we provide a condensed account of a variety of practitioner research traditions. There is only space to whet the reader's appetite to explore further the work summarized here. We hope that practitioners, armed with a knowledge of previous attempts to promote research by practitioners, will be in a better position to articulate the importance and legitimacy of their own work.

Beginnings of Practitioner Research

The idea of educational practitioners doing research in schools goes back at least as far as the late 19th and early 20th century, with the movement for the scientific study of education. Teachers were viewed as the front line of data gatherers for a massive research movement that saw teachers as researchers, working scientifically in their classroom-laboratories (McKernan, 1988).

Although this vision of teachers as researchers never materialized, it is interesting to note that within this model, teachers were allocated the role of carrying out research in their classrooms that was designed by university researchers. This vision of teachers as researchers viewed teachers as mere gatherers of data that could be analyzed statistically.

As early as 1926, Buckingham (cited in McKernan, 1988) recognized the potential of qualitative, case study research: "Among the many types of research work available to teachers, the making of case studies is by no means unimportant" (p. 176). The hierarchical relations between universities and schools reflected in most of this early work on practitioner research continues to be a source of tension today.

Overlapping this scientific movement in education was the progressive movement inspired by John Dewey. Referring to Dewey's contribution to action research, McKernan (1988) states:

> In *Logic: The Theory of Inquiry,* he once again argues that there must be a unity of the structure of inquiry in both common sense and science. He promoted logic as a method of scientific thinking and problem resolution. Later action researchers, such as Lewin, Corey, and Taba, also followed these steps of reflective thinking, thus demonstrating the linkage of the scientific method with action research. (p. 176)

In a more direct reference to practitioner research, Dewey (cited in McKernan, 1988) states:

> Educational practices provide the data, the subject matter which form the problems of enquiry. . . . A constant flow of less formal reports on special school affairs and results is needed. . . . It seems to me that the contributions that might come from classroom teachers are a comparatively neglected field; or, to change the metaphor, an almost unworked mine. (p. 177)

Dewey's work is the inspiration of much of the current writing on the "reflective practitioner" (Schon, 1983), which has helped us better understand how school practitioners make sense of their experiences and engage in professional learning. (For a more complete discussion of action research and the Progressive era, see Schubert & Schubert, 1984.)

The Action Research Tradition

Some see the origins of action research in the work of Lewin and the group-dynamics movement of the 1940s. Although Lewin was not the first to use or advocate action research, he was the first to develop a theory of action research that made it a respectable form of research in the social sciences. Lewin believed that knowledge should be created from problem solving in real-life situations. Among

the problems he studied were those related to production in facto-
ries and discrimination against minority groups (Lewin, 1946, 1948).
Argyris and Schon (1991) briefly describe the goals and methods of
the action research tradition:

> Action research takes its cues—its questions, puzzles, and
> problems—from the perceptions of practitioners within par-
> ticular, local practice contexts. It bounds episodes of research
> according to the boundaries of the local context. It builds
> descriptions and theories within the practice context itself,
> and tests them there through *intervention experiments*—that
> is, through experiments that bear the double burden of testing
> hypotheses and effecting some (putatively) desired change
> in the situation. (p. 86)

The double burden that Argyris and Schon refer to is the concern
with both action (improvement of practice, social change, and the
like) and research (creating valid knowledge about practice). According to them, this sets up a conflict between the rigor and the relevance of the research—a conflict that has been viewed as both an
advantage and a disadvantage by different commentators. Unlike
traditional social science research that frowns on intervening in any
way in the research setting, action research demands some form of
intervention. For the action researcher, this intervention constitutes
a spiral of action cycles in which one undertakes:

1. To develop a plan of action to improve what is already happening.
2. To act to implement the plan.
3. To observe the effects of action in the context in which it occurs.
4. To reflect on these effects as a basis for further planning and
   subsequent action through a succession of cycles. (Kemmis,
   1982, p. 7)

This cycle of activities forms an action research spiral in which
each cycle increases the researcher's knowledge of the original
question, puzzle, or problem, and leads to its solution.

Action Research in Education

During the early 1950s, action research was promoted in the field of education principally by Corey (1949, 1953, 1954) at Columbia Teachers College. Corey believed that teachers would likely find the results of their own research more useful than that of outsiders, and thus would be more likely to question current curricular practices. Corey was the executive officer of the Horace Mann-Lincoln Institute of School Experimentation, which was founded at Teachers College by H. L. Caswell. Under Corey's direction, members of the institute's staff collaborated on research with classroom teachers. In his 1953 book, Corey published several of these studies and a summary of what he called the "cooperative action research movement." Foshay (1993), a participant in the movement (Foshay & Wann, 1953), describes the rather sudden demise of action research in education:

> The chief limitation of cooperative action research, from the point of view of the educational researchers of the time, was that it was not possible to generalize from the examined population to others, because no attempt was made to see whether the examined population was representative of a larger population. In addition, since much of the research was designed and carried out by classroom teachers, who were not trained in research, the data often were flawed. For these reasons the movement was ridiculed in the publications of AERA, and it did not spread. It disappeared as the members of the Institute staff scattered with the passage of time. (Foshay, 1993, p. 3)

It is not surprising, given the general hostility that educational researchers in the 1950s felt toward nonpositivist research of any kind, that action research was ridiculed and judged by positivist standards. By the end of the 1950s, action research had declined not only in the field of education, but in the social sciences as well. Sanford (1970) suggests that funding agencies wanted more basic research, and that an increasing split between science and practice led to the cult of the expert (Lindblom & Cohen, 1979) and the top-down, "social engineering" mentality of the period.

Although it never totally disappeared, interest in action research waned during the 1960s—a decade in which adherence to the cult of social engineering reached its height. The late British researcher Lawrence Stenhouse is usually credited with renewing interest in action research in Britain during the 1970s.

The Teacher-as-Researcher Movement in Great Britain

Although there has been much discussion throughout the 20th century of the idea of school practitioners doing research within their own sites, there generally has been more talk than action. Although this is the case to some extent today, a teacher research movement that began in Great Britain during the late 1960s began to change this. This movement is most often associated with the work of Lawrence Stenhouse, who established the Center for Applied Research in Education (CARE) at East Anglia University, and later with the work of John Elliott and Clem Adelman of the Ford Teaching Project.

Elliott (1991) makes the case that teacher research began as a teacher-led curriculum reform movement that grew out of concern by teachers over the forced implementation of behavioral objectives in curriculum and Great Britain's tracked educational system. He describes his own participation in the teachers-as-researchers movement in Great Britian during the 1960s:

> Curriculum practices were not derived (by us) from curriculum theories generated and tested independently of that practice. They constituted means by which we generated and tested our own and each others' theories. Practices took on the status of hypotheses to be tested. So we collected empirical data about their effects, and used it as evidence in which to ground our theorizing with each other in the context of collegial accountability. We didn't call it research, let alone action research. This articulation came much later as the world of academia responded to change in schools. But the concept of teaching as reflexive practice and a form of educational inquiry was tacitly and intuitively grasped in our experience of the innovation process. Our research was by

no means systematic. It occurred as a response to particular questions and issues as they arose. (p. 8)

The heyday of action research in Great Britain saw a teacher research movement develop in the schools as well as a series of large, state-funded collaborative action research projects. During the 1970s and 1980s, a lively debate took place in Great Britain over a number of issues in action research. Among them were a search for a guiding paradigm (Altricher & Posch, 1989), the political problems of promoting action research within institutions that do not want to look at themselves too closely (Holly, 1989), and the usefulness of more quantitative approaches to action research (Harwood, 1991). One of the most interesting critiques was that of feminist action researchers.

Feminist researchers involved in the Girls and Occupational Choice Project (Chisholm, 1990; Weiner, 1989) and Girls in Science and Technology (Whyte, 1987) argue that action research was being turned into a project in social engineering and was losing its "emancipatory" potential. German feminist action researcher Mies (cited in Chisholm, 1990) argues that the radical potential of action research is lost when it is turned into a recipe and controlled by state agencies:

> [Early on] "action" was interpreted not as socially liberating and dynamic praxis, but rather, in a manner observable in many activist groupings where precise short-term goals are set, as a narrow pragmatism. The same would appear to be true for what is termed "action research," which typically comprises planned intervention in specific social contexts, mostly under the control and direction of state agencies and monitored by researchers—in other words, a sort of social engineering. (Chisholm, 1990, p. 255)

This concern with moving action research beyond narrow pragmatism and planned interventions by external agencies had been taken up earlier by a group of Australians led by Stephen Kemmis, who spent time with British action researchers at East Anglia (Tripp, 1990). Carr and Kemmis (1983) challenge older models of action research as essentially conservative and positivistic. In a later article,

Carr (1989) reasserts that, "in theory, action research is only intelligible as an attempt to revive those forms of democratic dialogue and reflective theorizing which under the impact of positivism have been rendered marginal" (p. 89). He is concerned that, as action research becomes more methodologically sophisticated and technically proficient, it will lose its critical edge.

Two booklets that are cited frequently by North American teacher researchers are Kemmis and McTaggart's *The Action Research Planner* (1982), a user-friendly introduction to the action research spiral, and Kemmis' *The Action Research Reader* (1982), a compilation of critical action research studies.

Participatory Research: The Legacy of Freire

Long before feminists and critical theorists began their critique of the conservatism of traditional action research models, a model of action research was taking hold in Latin America. After the Brazilian military coup of 1964, Paulo Freire, literacy worker and author of *Pedagogy of the Oppressed* (1970), went into exile in Chile. During the late 1960s and early 1970s, Freire and a group of Chilean literacy educators began a series of "thematic research" projects. Freire's (1970) notion of thematic research is a highly inductive process in which research is viewed as a form of social action. In this type of research, "generative themes," or issues of vital importance to community members, are identified; used as a basis for literacy instruction; and studied in a collaborative fashion. Such projects have a dual purpose: To help participants (usually adults) acquire literacy and to help them engage in social critique and social action. In other words, literacy involves learning to read the word and the world.

During the last two decades, this type of research, now more commonly called "participatory research," has been done all over Latin America and the rest of the third world (Brown & Tandon, 1983; Fals Borda, 1979; Fernandes & Tandon, 1981; Gaventa, 1988; Hall, 1981; Tandon, 1981; Yopo, 1984). A North American example of a similar approach is the work in Appalachia of the Highlander Center, led by Miles Horton and more recently by Gaventa (Gaventa & Horton, 1981).

Although methodological considerations depend on the context within which the study is undertaken, de Schutter and Yopo (1981, p. 68) describe the following as general characteristics of participatory research:

- The point of departure for participatory research is a vision of social events as contextualized by macrolevel social forces.
- Social processes and structures are understood within a historical context.
- Theory and practice are integrated.
- The subject-object relationship is transformed into a subject-subject relationship through dialogue.
- Research and action (including education itself) become a single process.
- The community and researcher together produce critical knowledge aimed at social transformation.
- The results of research are immediately applied to a concrete situation.

In Freirean-inspired participatory research, the academic research model is challenged at almost every point. The dualisms of theory and practice, subject and object, research and teaching, are collapsed. This perspective also challenges many of the premises of more traditional models of action research. Many of the criticisms are similar to the feminist critique of action research discussed above. Brown and Tandon (1983) indicate that traditional action research tends to concentrate on an individual or group level of analysis of problems, whereas participatory research, with its more emancipatory emphasis, tends to focus on a broader societal analysis. Traditional action research tends to emphasize issues of efficiency and improvement of practices, whereas participatory research is concerned with equity/self-reliance/oppression problems.

Participatory research also operates out of a more politically sophisticated perspective and is viewed as taking place within a field of power relations, in which conflicts of interest often create resistance to the research. Participatory researchers assume that they will be resisted from above (i.e., by powerful vested interests), whereas traditional action researchers are often consultants who are hired by the powerful.

Action Science

Action science is largely associated with the work of Argyris (Argyris, Putnam, & Smith, 1985), who has been influenced by the action research tradition discussed above. More recently, he has incorporated aspects of critical theory into his work, particularly Habermas' (1979) theory of communication, which seeks to establish nondistorted communication in which the force of the better argument prevails, as judged in free and open discussion.

Argyris wishes to return the scientific dimension to action research, arguing that the problem-solving focus of action research has moved it too far away from the tasks of theory building and testing. The goal of an action science, according to Argyris, is the generation of "knowledge that is useful, valid, descriptive of the world, and informative of how we might change it" (Argyris et al., 1985, p. x). He has criticized some types of action research for adhering to traditional social science notions of "rigorous research," arguing that "to attain a certain level of rigor, the methodology may become so disconnected from the reality it is designed to understand that it is no longer useful" (Argyris et al., 1985, p. x).

Drawing on the work of Dewey and Lewin, and often writing with Schon (Argyris & Schon, 1974), Argyris over the years has evolved an intervention strategy for changing the status quo that stresses organizational learning. According to Argyris et al. (1985):

> in social life, the status quo exists because the norms and rules learned through socialization have been internalized and are continually reinforced. Human beings learn which skills work within the status quo and which do not work. The more the skills work, the more they influence individuals' sense of competence. Individuals draw on such skills and justify their use by identifying the values embedded in them and adhering to these values. The interdependence among norms, rules, skills, and values creates a pattern called the status quo that becomes so omnipresent as to be taken for granted

and to go unchallenged. Precisely because these patterns are taken for granted, precisely because these skills are automatic, precisely because values are internalized, the status quo and individuals' personal responsibility for maintaining it cannot be studied without confronting it. (p. xi)

Argyris' work is important for practitioner researchers because it points out why many institutions may not be thrilled at the idea of close examination. It is also important because unless solutions to the classroom and school problems under study tap into the complex theories of action that underlie and maintain the status quo, problems will only be solved in a superficial and temporary manner.

Robinson (1993), a former student of Argyris, describes the need for problem-based methodology in educational research:

Much research has failed to influence educational problems because it has separated problematic practices from the pre-theorized problem-solving processes that gave rise to them and which render them sensible to those who engage in them. Once practice is understood in this way, the theorizing and reasoning of practitioners becomes a key to understanding what sustains problematic practice. Problem-based methodology provides a way of uncovering, evaluating and, if necessary, reconstructing these theories of action. (p. 256)

What Robinson's work implies is that practitioner research should not simply promote practitioners' "practical theories" (Sanders & McCutcheon, 1986) in a nonproblematic way, but should explore in self-reflective ways how some practical theories may be perpetuating the very problems practitioners identify for study.

The Teacher Researcher Movement in North America

Although the teacher researcher movement in North America occurred later than in Britain and Latin America, it was not derivative of either movement, nor was it a reappropriation of the North American action research movement of the 1940s and 1950s. The Center for Applied Research in Education at East Anglia in Great

Britain and the work of Freire inspired many North American academics and some teachers, but the movement among North American teachers to do research began with a unique set of circumstances.

1. The dominance of the quantitative, positivistic paradigm of research in education was challenged by qualitative, case study, and ethnographic research from the late 1960s on. Because they more closely resemble the narrative forms already used by practitioners to communicate their knowledge, making qualitative forms of research legitimate helped open the door for practitioners to experiment with more systematic qualitative approaches in studying their practice.

2. Research on successful school change efforts and schools as contexts for teachers' professional work began to report that school-based problem-solving approaches to change were more likely to be implemented successfully than large, federally funded, outside-in initiatives (Fullan, 1982; Lieberman & Miller, 1984). These findings spawned a large number of "collaborative" or "interactive" research and development efforts, in which educational practitioners were invited to work alongside R&D experts in implementing programs and improving practices. (For accounts of these collaborative research projects, see Griffin, Lieberman, & Jacullo-Noto, 1982; Huling & Johnson, 1983; Oakes, Hare, & Sirotnik, 1986; Oja & Ham, 1984; Ross, 1983; Tikunoff, Ward, & Griffin, 1979.)

3. The increased deskilling of teachers and the dissemination of teacher-proof curricula spawned an effort on the part of educational practitioners to reprofessionalize teaching and to reclaim teachers' knowledge about practice as valid. *The Reflective Practitioner*, by Donald Schon (1983) encourages practitioners to tap into their store of professional knowledge to make it explicit and share it with other practitioners. From the notion of "reflective practice," it was only a short step to that of practitioner research, which became linked to an overall attempt by educational practitioners to reassert their professionalism. The Boston Women's Teachers' Group's report, *The Effect of Teaching on Teachers* (Freedman, Jackson, & Boles, 1986) describes the structural conditions and

isolation of teachers' work that makes professionalism difficult (see also Freedman, Jackson, & Boles, 1983). This report points out that teachers work "in an institution which supposedly prepares its clients for adulthood, but which views those entrusted with this task as incapable of mature judgement" (Freedman, Jackson, & Boles, 1986, p. 263). Liston and Zeichner (1991), in reviewing the group's work, point out that the research was used to "combat the individualistic bias in the school reform movement of the 1980's, which served to direct teachers' sense of frustration with and anger about their work away from a critical analysis of schools as institutions to a preoccupation with their own individual failures" (p. 150). Increasingly, a connection is being made between practitioner research and the notion of professional renewal among school practitioners (McTaggart, 1989).

4. Encouraged by the pioneering work of Atwell (1982), Goswami and Stillman (1987), Graves (1981a, 1981b), Myers (1985), and the Bay Area Writing Project, teachers of writing led the way in doing teacher research and writing about it from an insider perspective. Not only have they used student writing as data, but they have written case studies of a variety of issues on the teaching of writing (see Belanger, 1992). Because of these teachers' commitment to writing, they have led the way in writing and publishing accounts of their experiences as teacher researchers. (See Bissex & Bullock, 1987; Goswami & Schultz, 1993; Literacies Institute, 1993; and Newkirk, 1992, for examples. See also our summary of Belanger's [1992] research in Chapter 3.)

5. Many university teacher education programs and university/ school collaborations began to emphasize teacher research. One of the best known efforts to incorporate teacher research into a teacher education program is that of Ken Zeichner and others at the University of Wisconsin (Liston & Zeichner, 1991). Susan Noffke, Jennifer Gore, and Marie Brennan, all former university supervisors in the elementary teacher education program at Wisconsin, have documented the uses of practitioner research in the training of teachers (Gore & Zeichner, 1991; Noffke & Brennan, 1991; Zeichner, 1981).

At the University of New Mexico, a group of cooperating teachers and student teachers facilitated by Michelle Raisch engaged in a series of collaborative practitioner research projects as part of their teacher training experience. The cooperating teachers became so enthusiastic about the research that they continued to engage in and write about their classroom research (Anderson, Butts, Lett, Mansdoerfer, & Raisch, 1992).

Programs of this kind are becoming more common in colleges of education and promise to have an important impact on moving teacher and administrative preparation programs toward a more reflective model. Other practitioner studies that were done as part of university-school collaborations are reported in detail in Chapter 3 (Christman, Hirshman, Holtz, Perry, Spelkoman, & Williams, in press; Gitlin et al., 1992; Soohoo, 1991). For accounts of other similar programs and discussions of the role of practitioner research in teacher education and school-university collaboration, see Broyles (1991); Kyle and Hovda (1987a, 1987b); Ross (1989); Rudduck (1985); Tom (1985); Wallat, Green, Conlin, and Haramis (1981); Whitford, Schlechty, and Shelor (1989); and Wood (1988).

6. More recently, the school restructuring movement has begun to propose restructuring schools to create conditions that nurture teacher inquiry and reflection. The Holmes Group's *Tomorrow's Schools* (1990) contains a chapter dedicated to schools as "centers for reflection and inquiry." This chapter covers themes first reported in *The School as a Center of Inquiry* by Schaefer (1967). Many states have initiated collaborative efforts to restructure schools and have included practitioner research as an aspect of teacher empowerment. In Georgia, the League of Professional Schools has made action research a key component in the move toward shared governance and school renewal (Calhoun & Glickman, 1993; Glickman & Allen, 1991). These types of statewide, university-based school improvement movements promise to make practitioner research more legitimate, while at the same time threaten to co-opt and domesticate it to mainstream goals and norms (see Calhoun, 1993; Ellwood, 1993; Faust, 1993; Feldman, 1992; Noffke & Stevenson, 1994; Reed & Williams, 1993).

Practitioner Research:
From Academic Tradition to Social Movement

Older traditions of action research were generally associated with academics, mostly social scientists and virtually all men—such as Dewey, Lewin, Corey, Stenhouse, Elliott, Argyris, Schon, Freire, and Kemmis. As school practitioners become more active in sharing their work and practitioner research becomes a broad-based movement, practitioner research has the potential to reject the dualistic hierarchies of university and school, knowledge and action, theory and practice. It has the potential to become a truly grassroots, democratic movement of knowledge production and educational and social change. Winter (1987) elaborates on how practitioner research challenges current conceptions of social inquiry:

> Action research addresses "head on" social inquiry's fundamental problems—the relation between theory and practice, between the general and the particular, between common sense and academic expertise, between mundane action and critical reflection, and hence—ultimately—between ideology and understanding. (p. viii)

However, there are dangers in assuming this process will happen without struggle. Some commentators promote teacher research as inherently progressive and as leading to emancipatory change in education:

> When teachers do research, they draw on interpretive frameworks built from their histories and intellectual interests, and because the research process is embedded in practice, the relationship between knower and known is significantly altered. This obviates the need to "translate findings" in the conventional sense and moves teacher research toward praxis, or critical reflection on practice (Lather, 1986). . . . In this different epistemology, teacher research currently marginalized in the field, would contribute to a fundamental reconceptualization of knowledge for teaching. Through inquiry,

teachers would play a role in reinventing the conventions
of interpretive social science, just as feminist researchers and
critical ethnographers have done by making problematic
the relationships of researcher and researched, knowledge
and authority, and subject and object (Crawford & Marecek,
1989; Noffke, 1990). (Cochran-Smith & Lytle, 1993, p. 43)

Although practitioner knowledge may acquire greater acceptance as valid knowledge and cease to be marginalized, the impli-
cation that this alternative knowledge base will represent critical
reflection or the kind of emancipatory praxis that Lather (1986) describes is unsubstantiated. Cochran-Smith and Lytle (1993), unlike
the more critically oriented researchers they cite, do not explore how
teachers' interpretive frameworks, histories, and intellectual interests represent social constructions, in most cases constructed out of
the technical rationality (Schon, 1983) that permeates the society in
which we live and the social institutions in which we are trained and
work. Their optimism about the teacher research movement becoming an independent and oppositional movement, like that of femi-
nism or critical ethnography, appears ungrounded in an understanding of the potential barriers.

Kincheloe (1991) presents an alternative possibility:

When the critical dimension of teacher research is negated,
the teacher-as-researcher movement can become quite a trivial
enterprise. Uncritical educational action research seeks direct applications of information gleaned to specific situations—a cookbook style of technical thinking is encouraged
. . . . Such thinking does not allow for complex reconceptu-
alizations of knowledge and as a result fails to understand
the ambiguities and the ideological structures of the classroom. [In this way] teacher research is co-opted, its democratic edge is blunted. It becomes a popular grassroots
movement that can be supported by the power hierarchy—
it does not threaten, nor is it threatened. Asking trivial
questions, the movement presents no radical challenge or

offers no transformative vision of educational purpose, as
it acts in ignorance of deep structures of schooling. (p. 83)

In a similar vein, Miller (1990) recounts how she and a group of
teachers in a research study group struggled with this very issue of
expanding the focus of practitioner research so as to become "chal-
lengers" of nonresponsive educational institutions. One teacher
researcher in the group asks the following question:

Do you think that we could just turn into another form, an
acceptable professional form of empowerment? Well, what
I mean is that nothing would please some administrators I
know more than to think that we were doing "research" in
their terms. That's what scares me about the phrase "teacher-
as-researcher" these days—too packaged. People buy back
into the very system that shuts them down. That immediately eliminates the critical perspectives that we're working
on, I'm afraid. But I'm still convinced that if enough people
do this, we could get to a point of seeing at least a bigger
clearing for us. (p. 114)

As Schon (1983) points out, social institutions are characterized
by dynamic conservatism. This conservatism is dynamic in that it
constantly pulls practitioners back to a status quo that, as noted by
Argyris et al. (1985), consists of norms, rules, skills, and values that
become so omnipresent as to be taken for granted and to go unchallenged. Practitioner research either can reproduce those norms, rules,
skills, and values or it can challenge them. However, practitioners
intuitively know that when they challenge the norms, the institutions'
dynamic conservatism will respond in a defensive, self-protective
manner.

If the practitioner research movement is to break out of the dynamic
conservatism of schools and school systems, then these institutional
issues must be addressed by practitioner researchers; as Miller
(1990) indicates, this may be best done in the context of practitioner
research study groups.

A teacher in Miller's group wonders whether, as teachers find their voices through critical forms of practitioner research, their schools will welcome their voices or view them as troublemakers:

What's bothering me still is what's beneath the apparent. What's bothering me is not really the idea of no copy machine for teachers to use, or mice in the school, or the lack of supplies. I've finally realized that teaching is a political thing. Its politics remain under the table. I know that I have deliberately and consciously avoided this for many years. I can honestly say that I was aware of it but chose to remain removed, naive, and ill-informed. When I started in 1977, I told myself that I'd never be involved. So I taught each and every class with exactly what I was given, did exactly what I was told. I never questioned class size, supply procedures, curriculum requirements or extracurricular demands. I volunteered for everything from spring concert, to participating in Gym night, to working in three schools with no time for a scheduled lunch period. But, now I'm no longer willing to do all of that, or at least I now ask "why?" I know that I'm different now than I used to be as a teacher, I know I'm thinking differently, I *know* that I'm involved, because teaching *is* involvement! I know my involvement, my becoming vocal, has been noticed. And I don't think they like it! But I can no longer be the teacher who just teaches what others have thought up and given name to. I'm running things now. What about me as an *educator?* Can there be such a thing, can I exist? (p. 140)

Practitioners must make their peace with how much of a challenger of the status quo they wish to be. Some are more skillful and in stronger positions to take stands on issues than others. However, if practitioner research is not done with a critical spirit, it runs the risk of legitimating what may be—from the perspective of equity considerations—unacceptable social arrangements.

Practitioner Research: Epistemology

Is Practitioner Research a "Valid" Way of Knowing?

We phrase the above question in terms of validity, not because we wish to adopt positivistic language for practitioner research, but because practitioners are often confronted with it in such terms. *Internal validity* is generally defined as the trustworthiness of inferences drawn from data. *External validity* refers to how well these inferences generalize to a larger population or are transferable to other contexts. Because most academic educational researchers are part of a positivistic tradition inherited from the natural sciences via the discipline of psychology, they consider the notion of validity to be of utmost importance in educational research. The more recent influence of ethnography and qualitative case study methods has tempered this tendency. Because qualitative researchers have developed their own set of rules about the "validity" of qualitative research findings, we will review these rules before proposing new ones for practitioner research.

Although qualitative researchers are not in total agreement, they generally reject the claims of positivism that research is fundamentally about pursuing truth value (internal validity) by demonstrating that causes and their effects have been isolated. Lincoln and Guba (1985) propose that the comparable standard of "trustworthiness" is more appropriate for naturalistic (i.e., qualitative) inquiry. A study's trustworthiness involves the demonstration that the researcher's interpretations of the data are credible or "ring true" to those who provided the data.

Although the standards for qualitative inquiry are different than those used by quantitative researchers, they may not be appropriate for practitioner researchers. This is partly because qualitative researchers tend to be outsiders studying settings in which they are not true participants; practitioner researchers are insiders studying their own setting.

In many ways, the two groups have opposite dilemmas. Academics (outsiders) want to understand what it is like to be an insider without "going native" and losing the outsider's perspective. Practitioners (insiders) already know what it is like to be an insider, but because they are "native" to the setting, they must work to see the taken-for-granted aspects of their practice from an outsider's perspective. This is further complicated by the fact that many academic researchers have, in fact, been school practitioners (as well as having experienced schools as a student) and are, therefore, in some sense both insiders and outsiders. Moreover, many school practitioners have been socialized into academic research through graduate study and have internalized many outsider social categories. Therefore, the distance between university researchers/practitioners and school practitioners/researchers is sometimes not as great as we make it to be in theory.

To make things even more complex, qualitative researchers do not always agree among themselves about the purposes of research and criteria for validity. For example, some qualitative researchers prefer a more interventionist, emancipatory approach to qualitative research. Because of the more traditional qualitative researchers' "fly on the wall" approach to school and classroom observation, some critical and feminist researchers claim that qualitative research is mired in positivism, in that it "affirms a social world that is meant to be gazed upon but not challenged or transformed" (Roman, 1992, p. 573).

In spite of some common experiences with schooling and an openness to collaboration, the cultures of the university research community and that of school practitioners are characterized by very different purposes, norms, views of valid knowledge, and work conditions. For instance, the purposes of academic qualitative research and practitioner research are fundamentally different. Qualitative research belongs to the knowledge creation/dissemination/utilization model of applied knowledge, whereas most practitioner research is utilized in the same setting in which it is created. Clearly, more honest communication between these cultures is required for true collaboration.

Green and Chandler (1990) suggest that the divisions are even more complex than those we have described, and propose that dialogue must occur

> both across groups of inquirers as well as within groups.
> Researchers, practitioners, and policymakers need to develop

strategies for engaging in a dialog[ue] about practice as will researchers of differing perspectives and practitioners and policymakers with differing perspectives, goals and positions. In other words, all educators need to develop a conversation of practice. (p. 214)

We support this notion of dialogue and hope that practitioners will soon be accepted into it as equals. Nevertheless, practitioner researchers are well advised to think through the epistemological implications of insider research in which knowledge utilization and creation alternate as action informs theory and theory informs action with the goal of understanding and changing practice. In this type of research, academic conceptions of validity, whether quantitative or qualitative, are of limited use to the practitioner researcher.

If practitioner researchers are to be accepted in a larger dialogue about education, they must develop some inquiry criteria for their research. This is not to say that they need to justify themselves by the same inquiry criteria as academic research, but rather that they must make the case for a different conception of validity. This conception of validity should respond to the purposes and conditions of practitioner research and the uniqueness of its contribution to the dialogue.

The very condition of being a teacher requires a certain appreciation for the differences between rigorous and sloppy work, between analysis and mere opinion. Educational practitioners routinely apply these criteria to their students' work, and there is no reason to believe they would resist applying it to their own and each others' work. In fact, as we discuss below, the project of defining inquiry criteria for practitioner research is currently underway.

Criteria for "Validity" in Practitioner Research

As we mention in Chapter 1, practitioners do research in their sites for different reasons. If the purpose of practitioner research is to produce knowledge for dissemination in fairly traditional channels (e.g., dissertations, journals), then the criteria for a "valid" study may be different than the criteria of practitioners who organize their research around specific problems within an action context.

Furthermore, whereas social science research often fetishizes method, practitioner research is less dependent on research method for its validity criteria. Less dependence causes what Greene (1992) identifies as "a blurring of the boundaries between ways of knowing offered by social science and by literature and other humanities" (p. 41).

The following criteria are tentative, and they are best applied to action research that is transformative in nature (i.e., research that is linked to some kind of action to change educational and/or institutional practices).

Democratic Validity

To what extent is the research done in collaboration with all parties who have a stake in the problem under investigation? If not done collaboratively, how are multiple perspectives and material interests taken into account in the study? For example, are teachers and/or administrators, through practitioner research, finding solutions to problems that benefit them at the expense of other stakeholders? Are students and their parents seen as part of the insider community that undertakes this type of research, or are they viewed as outsiders by practitioner researchers?

Another version of democratic validity is what Cunningham (1983) calls "local" validity, in which the problems emerge from a particular context and solutions are appropriate to that context. Watkins (1991) calls this "relevancy" or "applicability" criteria for validity (i.e., "How do we determine the relevance of findings to the needs of the problem context?") (p. 15).

Outcome Validity

According to Cunningham (1983), one test of the validity of action research is the extent to which actions occur that lead to a resolution of the problem under study. In this sense, validity is synonymous with the "successful" outcome of the research project. This begs the question raised in the section on democratic validity: successful for whom? Moreover, it ignores the fact that most good research, rather than simply solving a problem, forces us to reframe the problem in a more complex way, often leading to a new set of questions/problems.

Nevertheless, the notion of validity as successfully completing an action research spiral of problem solving seems to makes sense. Watkins (1991) points out that "many action research studies abort at the stage of diagnosis of a problem or the implementation of a single solution strategy, irrespective of whether or not it resolves the presenting problem" (p. 8).

Process Validity

In discussing the process of action research, Watkins (1991) refers to the "dependability" and "competency" of the study. She raises the question, "To what extent are we able to determine the adequacy of the process and are problems solved in a manner that permits ongoing learning of the individual or system?" (see Argyris et al., 1985). Outcome validity, therefore, is dependent on process validity. If the process is superficial or flawed, the outcome will reflect it.

Whereas democratic validity depends on the inclusion of multiple voices as a social justice issue, the notion of triangulation, or the inclusion of multiple perspectives, guards against viewing events in a simplistic or biased way. Triangulation also can refer to using a variety of methods—for example, observation and interviews—so that a researcher is not limited to only one kind of data source.

Process is not, however, limited to method. In narrative and essayist forms of inquiry, there are distinct criteria for what makes a good empirical narrative (as opposed to fiction). Connelly and Clandinin (1990) warn that, "not only may one 'fake the data' and write a fiction but one may also use the data to tell a deception as easily as a truth" (p. 10). Thus, criteria, like verisimilitude, plausibility, and intention, become important for judging narratives. (See Connelly & Clandinin, 1990, for an elaboration of these criteria.)

Catalytic Validity

Catalytic validity is "the degree to which the research process reorients, focuses, and energizes participants toward knowing reality in order to transform it" (Lather, 1986, p. 272). In the case of practitioner research, not only the participants, but the researchers themselves must be open to reorienting their view of reality as well as their view of their practitioner role. All involved in the research should deepen their understanding of the social reality under study and should be moved to some action to change it. The most powerful practitioner research studies are those in which the practitioners recount a change in their own and their participants' understandings.

This reinforces the importance of the role of a research journal, in which practitioner researchers can monitor their own change process and consequent changes in the dynamics of the setting. For example, Richards' (1989) account of the "bums" of 8H includes powerful examples from her reflective journal documenting her changing sense of her role and her changing perceptions of her students.

Dialogic Validity

In academic research the "goodness" of research is monitored through peer review. Research reports must pass through the process of peer review to be disseminated through academic journals. Many academic journals even provide opportunities for researchers to engage in point/counterpoint debates about research. A similar form of peer review is beginning to develop within and among practitioner research communities. Many practitioner research groups are forming throughout North America, as practitioner researchers seek dialogue with peers.

To promote both democratic and dialogic validity, some insist that practitioner research should only be done as collaborative inquiry (Torbert, 1981). Others suggest that practitioner researchers participate in critical and reflective dialogue with other practitioner researchers (Martin, 1987) or work with a critical friend who is familiar with the setting and can serve as devil's advocate for alternative explanations of research data. When the dialogic nature of practitioner inquiry is stressed, studies can achieve what Myers (1985) calls "goodness-of-fit with the intuitions of the teacher community, both in its definition of problems and in its findings" (p. 5).

These validity criteria for practitioner research are tentative and in flux. We agree with Connelly and Clandinin (1990), who, in discussing validity criteria for narrative inquiry, state, "We think a variety of criteria, some appropriate to some circumstances and some to others, will eventually be the agreed-upon norm. It is currently the case that each inquirer must search for, and defend, the criteria that best apply to his or her work" (p. 7).

Are the Findings of Practitioner Research Generalizable?

There are many ways to approach the question of generalizability (external validity) of practitioner research, but we suggest one taken from the work of Stake (1986) on naturalistic generalization. Although Stake developed this approach in the context of outsider researchers creating more useful research for practitioners, we feel it has powerful implications for practitioner researchers. Stake's concept of naturalistic generalization is similar in many ways to Lincoln and Guba's (1985) notion of "transferability," in which findings are not generalized, but rather transferred from a sending context to a receiving context. According to Lincoln and Guba,

> if there is to be transferability, the burden of proof lies less with the original investigator than with the person seeking to make an application elsewhere. The original inquirer cannot know the sites to which transferability might be sought, but the appliers can and do. The best advice to give to anyone seeking to make a transfer is to accumulate *empirical* evidence about contextual similarity; the responsibility of the original investigator ends in providing sufficient descriptive data to make such similarity judgements possible. (p. 298)

Although similar to the notion of transferability, Stake's (1986) elaboration of naturalistic generalization is more closely tied to educational *action* and therefore serves our purposes here better.

After years of well-documented failure by outside experts to bring about planned change in schools, Stake (1986) argues that it is time to rediscover the lessons about change that Dewey (1916) taught us:

> Almost absent from mention in the "change literature" is the common way in which improvement is accomplished, a way

followed intuitively by the greatest, and the least, of our thinkers. It is the experiential way, an evolutionary way, recognized particularly by John Dewey. One may change practice when *new experience* causes re-examination of problems: Intuitively we start thinking of alternative solutions. (p. 90)

Stake also cites the work of Polanyi (1958) and Schon (1983), who argue that practice is guided less by formal knowledge than by personal knowledge based on personal or vicarious experience. They also argue that resistance to change is often a form of personal protection.

Stake's argument stipulates that action or change in educational practice usually occurs as a result of either some kind of external demand or coercion or the conviction on the part of practitioners that an action or change is necessary. We have seen time and again how coercion is successfully resisted by practitioners, and how most lasting change takes place through internal conviction, or to use a more popular term, "ownership."

A further premise is that a practitioner's internal conviction is influenced by a mixture of personal understanding and personal feeling or faith (voluntarism). Understanding, a primary goal of practitioner research, is arrived at through dialogue and reflection drawing on two kinds of knowledge: experiential and propositional. These two kinds of knowledge, according to Stake (1986), are tied to two kinds of generalization: formalistic and naturalistic. "Continuing the analysis, we might say that theory and codified data are the main constituents of our formal, verbalized generalizations—whereas experience, real and vicarious, is the main constituent of the naturalistic generalizations" (p. 97).

To summarize this highly condensed chain of influence, *action* is influenced by *internal conviction*, which comes from voluntarism and *personal understanding*. This, in turn, is achieved by both formal and *naturalistic generalization*, the latter being the result of direct and *vicarious experience*. In other words, practitioners tend to find traditional educational research, which is based on formalistic generalizations, less useful than narrative accounts from schools and classrooms that provide them with vicarious experience. Stake (1986) describes how naturalistic generalization is different from more traditional, formalistic generalization:

> The intention of most educational research is to provide for-
> malistic generalization. A typical research report might high-
> light the correlation between time spent on team projects
> *and* gain in scores on an achievement test. The report might
> identify personality, affective, and demographic variables.
> Even with little emphasis on causation this report is part of
> the grand explanation of student learning. It provides one
> way of knowing about educational practice.
>
> A more naturalistic research report might deal with the
> same topic, perhaps with the same teachers and pupils, yet
> reflecting a different epistemology. The naturalistic data
> would describe the actual interactions within student teams.
> The report would probably report project work—conveying
> style, context, and evolution. A person would be described
> as an individual, with uniqueness not just in deviance scores,
> but as a key to understanding the interactions. A reader senses
> the experience of teamwork in this particular situation. It is
> a *unique* situation in some respects, but ordinary in other
> respects. Readers recognize similarities with situations of
> their own. Perhaps they are stimulated to think of old prob-
> lems in a new way. (pp. 98-99)

This type of research fits well with the current practitioner culture where, although less systematic, stories are shared daily among
school practitioners as part of an oral craft tradition. According to
Holland (1992), "Stories have their own kind of power to engage the
mind of the reader or listener. As Bruner has described it, this power
resides in the ability of narrative, as a distinct mode of cognitive
functioning, to establish 'not truth, but verisimilitude' (Bruner, 1986,
p. 11)" (p. 200).

Likewise, Mishler (1986) suggests that the structure of the story
is built into the human mind much like the structures of grammar,
and humans make sense of and express their understanding of
events and experiences largely through narratives.

We have limited our discussion in this section to certain issues relating to what positivists call the internal and external validity of practitioner research. There are many other issues; issues such as how
practitioner research generates, tests, or extends educational theory,
or to what extent practitioner studies can and should be replicated
by other practitioners. However, to dwell on epistemological issues
means sacrificing space given for providing examples of what teacher
research looks like and how it is done. These are the themes of the
chapters that follow. First, however, we will discuss how doing practitioner research in schools can become a highly politicized enterprise.

Practitioner Research: Politics

The Politics of Knowledge,
Institutional Change, and Professionalism

One of the underlying assumptions of this book is that practitioner
research is best viewed as a vehicle for the empowerment of practitioners, students, and communities toward a goal of institutional
and social change from the inside. We feel that the vision of practitioner research as a packaged in-service promoted by external reformers or of isolated individual practitioners pursuing research in
static classrooms and schools is neither appealing nor desirable. Practitioner research, perhaps more than other innovations, must challenge the sociopolitical status quo of the setting. For practitioners to
resist falling into "sanitized" forms of practitioner research, we must
explore both the ways in which schools are themselves political and
the functions that schools serve in a broader sociopolitical context.
We do this not to discourage practitioners from engaging in research, but to help them understand the resistance they may encounter from some superordinates and peers. When practitioner research
is done skillfully and with the welfare of students at the center of
the research, tremendous benefits are likely to accrue to all involved.

What Is "Politics?"

When we talk about the "politics" of site-based research, we
mean several things. First, as practitioner research moves beyond

the four walls of the classroom, there is a need to understand the institutional micropolitical forces that practitioners will encounter. This institutional aspect of practitioner research has been generally glossed over in most of the literature.

Second, as school practitioners begin to redefine their roles as professional educators, they must critique the narrowness of current definitions of their roles. The work of educational practitioners is becoming more fragmented, more supervised, more assessed, and consequently more controlled from the outside. The attempt to gain control over and redefine one's profession is an essentially political move.

Third, the question of who creates knowledge about teaching, administering, and counseling is a political question. Time and again we hear how inaccessible and irrelevant most of the knowledge created by outside researchers is for educational practitioners. Much of what practitioners know about their practice is "subjugated knowledge" (Foucault, 1980), or knowledge that is not viewed as valid by those who create knowledge in universities and those who make educational policy.

We live in a time when subjugated knowledge is being brought to light. Women's studies programs and various ethnic studies programs are demanding legitimacy for diverse cultural and gendered ways of knowing. The knowledge of school practitioners and their students is a form of subjugated knowledge because it is not given legitimacy by those who make educational policy.

Fourth, underlying all these political aspects of practitioner research is the ultimate need to problematize many of the purposes or "functions" of various educational practices and of schooling as a social institution. We discuss each of these issues in greater detail in the remainder of this section.

Institutional Micropolitics

When teachers or principals say that their school or district is "political," they are usually talking about what we call here "micropolitics." Micropolitics includes behind-the-scenes negotiations over material resources, vested interests, and ideological commitments. The micropolitical struggles in many schools are over such issues as mainstreaming special education students, whole language versus basal reading instruction, academic tracking, and bilingual and multicultural education. More often, micropolitical struggles are over such things as professional jealousy, student class placements, parent-teacher relations, office or classroom space, hall duty, and gender and racial politics. Micropolitics is what gets talked about in private among teachers; it is also what never gets talked about because it is too "political." Micropolitics often exists within the silences created in educational institutions. It is as much about what does not get said as it is about what does.

Because of the essentially political nature of life in schools (and school districts), educational practitioners who are engaged in research in their schools are not necessarily welcomed with open arms by colleagues and administrators. Often they may feel threatened by potential "side effects" of practitioner research. Given its potential for moving beyond the study site and challenging power relations, practitioner research should not be undertaken ingenuously.

Often these side effects occur even when the research has been carefully contained within the four walls of the classroom. One middle school teacher found that when she began interviewing her students and engaged them in a collaborative study of their own classroom, the students started asking similar questions of teachers in other classrooms. This caught other teachers off guard and they correctly attributed it to the teacher's research project. Practitioner research, like all good qualitative research, has a natural tendency to spill over into areas one had not expected to study. For example, practitioners should expect that pursuing questions about one's classroom will inevitably lead to questions about the institutional context within which classrooms are embedded. Questions raised at the level of the school site will inevitably lead to questions about school district policies and central office politics. Qualitative research is by nature holistic, and therefore it cannot easily be used to study a phenomenon independent of the various layers of its social context.

The institutional politics of practitioner research rub up against what Schon (1971, cited in Holly, 1989) calls the "dynamic conservatism" of social institutions. According to Schon:

A social system is a complex of individuals which tends to maintain its boundaries and its patterns of internal relationships. But given internal tendencies towards increasing disorder, and external threats to stability, energy must be expended if the patterns of the system are to be held stable. Social systems are self-reinforcing systems which strive to remain in something like equilibrium. . . . Social systems resist change with an energy roughly proportional to the radicalness of the change that is threatened. (p. 80)

Practitioner researchers who work in schools are often ill-prepared for resistance (sometimes in the form of indifference) to their efforts. They encounter a school and district culture that values individual effort, professional isolation, and conformity (Anderson, 1991).

Hutchinson and Whitehouse (1986) describe the encounter between the practitioner researcher and institutional politics in the following terms:

While action research fosters collegiality, informality, openness, and collaboration, action researchers have to contend with educational institutions that are structured hierarchically with formal asymmetrical relations of power and responsibility. These, seen as polar tendencies, contribute to the struggle between two "political" realities where, usually, the action research project is . . . emasculated, neutralized, cut down to size by and within the institution. (p. 85)

These authors argue that practitioners who engage in research must deal not only with institutional politics but also with how their research contradicts the ways in which most practitioners define "professional competence." Referring to teachers, they state:

Confined to the narrow social context of the classroom a teacher's professional experience and her notions of professional competence are defined by the immediate curricular responsibilities and the practical matters of teaching and learning. . . . The action researcher has to re-assess reality

and commit herself to the notion that social reality is culturally created and contains contradictions of truth and value.
In accepting this, and in attempting to involve others in a
critique of practice (and all that this implies) she soon encounters resistance from those who understand their professional competence to be a positive and direct outcome of
the social reality that is confined to the classroom but cut off
from the wider social and political contexts. (p. 93)

Teachers, in particular, live in a fishbowl. Their professional
competence is constantly vulnerable to question from parents, students, principals, and fellow teachers. They are understandably defensive about what they may perceive as attacks on their professional
competence. Once practitioner researchers have conquered their
own fears about engaging in a social and cultural critique of their
own practices, they should expect many of their fellow practitioners
to view such a critique as a threat to their own fragile sense of professional competence. This broadening through inquiry into one's own
practice of what it means to be "competent" leads us to also rethink
what it means to be a professional.

The Politics of Redefining Professionalism

Practitioner research has been suggested as a way to reprofessionalize educational practice, particularly teaching, in the face
of increasing attempts to standardize and deskill teachers' work
(Cochran-Smith & Lytle, 1993). We will briefly explore what it has
meant historically for educational practitioners to gain professional
status and what it might mean today for practitioners to rethink
what it means to be a professional.

There are many excellent historical accounts of how educational
practitioners gained professional status. Gitlin et al. (1992), in a recent
attempt to condense much of this literature, demonstrate how the
move to gain professional legitimation has actually intensified
the divisions between educational research and practice. As normal
schools and teachers' colleges were abandoned in favor of university status, colleges of education increasingly adopted the arts and

sciences' definitions of valid knowledge over that of educational practitioners. According to Gitlin et al. (1992):

> Challenges to the normal school were based on both their practice emphasis and the inclusion of women in those institutions. To achieve professional status required not only a move away from practice toward scientific research, but also a move to differentiate the work of teachers, commonly seen as women's work, from the educational leadership positions held mostly by men. (p. 80)

The quest for professionalization also created a hierarchy between universities and public schools. Academics were viewed as creating valid knowledge about education, and so these "experts" were allotted time for research. They were also able to institute a system of peer governance in which questions of tenure, retention, and promotion were decided by colleagues.

The role of practitioner research in the politics of redefining professionalism is a continuation of this history. It is encouraging to see academic journals and the Holmes Group (1990) calling for "schools as centers of inquiry" and "teachers as communities of learners." However, until academics are willing to address the material conditions of teachers' work and help bring these worlds closer together, their promotion of practitioner research will sound hollow.

Ironically, the renewed interest in the professionalization of teachers has arrived at a time of a crisis of confidence in the professions generally. According to Schon (1983),

> when leading professionals write or speak about their own crisis of confidence, they tend to focus on the mismatch of traditional patterns of practice and knowledge to features of the practice situation—complexity, uncertainty, instability, uniqueness, and value conflict—of whose importance they are becoming increasingly aware. (p. 18)

This crisis of confidence comes, in part, from trying to force a definition of professionalism that values problem solving over problem framing, scientific knowledge over personal knowledge, and facts over values onto an educational reality that is messy, intuitive, anecdotal, and value laden. As reflective models of practice replace the old social engineer and craft models of practice, a practitioner research model of professionalism gains validity.

Finally, some educational practitioners have attempted to broaden the notion of "professional" to include more of an advocacy stance toward social issues related to education. This is really an old debate begun by "social reconstructionists" like Counts (1932), who argues that because democracy has to be recreated by each new generation, it is the task of educators to help young people reconstruct society rather than adapt to it. An example of teachers taking a strong advocacy position is the creation by Rita Tenorio and Bob Peterson of *Rethinking Schools*, a widely read newspaper developed to "shake up every teacher in the system, including the union leadership . . . by offering a vision of what we think should take place in the public schools" (Diegmueller, 1992, p. 26). Although not all attempts at social transformation are as ambitious nor as successful, the tendency of educators to view themselves as apolitical often keeps them from thinking—even at the classroom level—in ways that challenge the status quo.

The Politics of Educational Knowledge

Who creates knowledge about education, how it is created, and who uses it for what purposes are all political questions. Many see practitioner research as a social movement in which practitioners are attempting to assert their own ways of knowing educational and organizational processes as valid knowledge. In postmodern terms, the knowledge of educational practitioners, along with the knowledge of other marginalized groups like women, the poor, and some ethnic and racial groups, is subjugated knowledge. The problems of educational practice have always been framed by those who do not work in schools. Educational practitioners have traditionally been portrayed in the literature on educational reform as childlike creatures who foolishly resist attempts to bring about changes based on research done in universities and research and development centers.

Educational planners think in terms of knowledge created outside of schools, disseminated or diffused into schools, where it is implemented or utilized by practitioners. Planners hope this process will result in the institutionalization of their research-backed innovations. Reformers are now realizing that including practitioners in these efforts through collaborative action research projects is a more appropriate way to proceed, but many practitioners fear that this is just a more sophisticated implementation strategy. Rather than be empowered by outsiders, many practitioners are arguing that they must assert their own claims to the creation of legitimate knowledge. Rather than be invited to participate in projects initiated in universities and R&D centers, they want to initiate the projects and invite those outsiders with specialized knowledge to participate.

However, as educational practitioners move to reassert their professional prerogatives, they must be sensitive to others, such as parents, who are in their own way "experts" about their children, and students, who are also "experts" about their own experiences and needs. Although educational practitioners may rightly feel oppressed in their work conditions, the most oppressed groups are students, who are relatively powerless organizational members, and poor and minority parents, whose children live in marginalized communities.

For this reason, practitioners are advised to include students and parents in their research whenever possible and should be willing to submit their own cherished beliefs (even "progressive" ones) to examination when their students and communities question them. For example, Delpit (1986) has found, through critical reflection on her experience as a classroom teacher, that proponents of a whole language approach to the teaching of reading have in many cases done a disservice to poor, African American children, who, she argues, may benefit from a skills approach. Moreover, although many practitioners argue compellingly that standardized testing is tying their hands and deforming their curriculum, many advocates for poor communities argue that test scores are currently the only tool they have to hold the institutions that educate their children accountable. One of the lessons of qualitative research is that all educational practices are context bound, and that what might be effective or appropriate in one context might be ineffective or inappropriate in another.

The Politics of Schooling as a Social Institution

As practitioners generate questions for inquiry, these questions will not only spill over the boundaries of their classrooms into other classrooms and the school as a whole, they will also generate broader questions that reflect broader social issues. It is difficult to ask questions about ability grouping, for example, without asking to what extent one might be participating in a social tracking system. Most of the dilemmas that educators encounter in their schools and classroom reflect broader social dilemmas (Berlak & Berlak, 1981). This should be self-evident, since schools are obviously social institutions in the sense that they are created by and reflective of the society in which they are embedded, but most educational practitioners have been socialized not to think in this way. As social institutions, schools are stages on which many of our social dramas—from racial integration to occupational sorting (tracking)—are acted out. Some types of questions may seem more political than others, but any question we ask about educational practices in schools is necessarily political. We often attempt to frame questions about schools as if they were not social institutions that reflect a wide variety of vested interests and ideological commitments.

Conclusion

This chapter may have raised the anxiety levels of budding practitioner researchers. We hope, however, that it may head off any unrealistic expectations of doing neat and tidy studies in a political vacuum. We also hope it has freed practitioners from the burden of having to follow rigid research procedures encountered in universities. As Greene (1992) points out, the real issue for practitioners is less "getting it right" than "making it meaningful" (p. 39). In other words, practitioner research is about deepening our understanding of school life in the service of students. This is the goal of many critical thinking practitioners. Practitioner research can be a vehicle toward that end.

In Chapters 3 and 4, we provide examples of practitioners struggling with the various issues raised in this chapter. In Chapter 3, we attempt to give the reader a sense of the diversity of research that practitioners have undertaken. We have chosen studies that we feel exemplify the inquiry criteria discussed above. In Chapter 4, we provide a case study of coauthor Herr's research to illustrate the complexities of teacher research with a goal of empowerment.

3

What Does Practitioner Research Look Like?

When reviewing examples of practitioner research, it becomes readily apparent that approaches are wide ranging, from informal observations to highly formalized research projects; in short, there is no one "right" way to approach the issue of studying one's own practice site. Chism, Sanders, and Zitlow (1989) suggest that practitioners are constantly engaged informally in practice-centered inquiry:

> We recognized that teachers naturally do seem to use a form of inquiry to help deal with the problematic realities of teaching. It is a process that has not often been articulated but is familiar in the experience of many. In a given situation, effective teachers often: (a) Consider the situation based on the information available to them as participants in this particular teaching-learning process and select some action (a practice) tentatively based on their understanding of what is educationally desirable in that situation, feasible and likely to be effective in the sense of resulting in desired outcomes;

(b) Try out the practice and observe its results; and (c) Revise the practice if necessary, correct for flaws observed and try it again. (p. 2)

Practitioner research translates this type of informal questioning of practice to one of more systematic inquiry that lends itself to problem solving as well as possible dissemination to a larger audience.

The following examples should not be perceived as exhaustive in terms of the work currently being done by practitioner researchers. Although more research accounts by practitioners are appearing in print, there is still more incentive and opportunity for university-affiliated researchers and collaborators to disseminate their work in a broader arena; practitioner researchers more often enter the research process as a means of solving their own practice dilemmas or questions rather than to contribute to the field of education as a whole. Many site-based educators never consider writing a professional paper (Bailey et al., 1988) and, as Oberg and McCutheon (1987) point out, the rewards of publication may be outweighed for teachers by the time and energy required to prepare their research for the publication process. In a sense, this leaves the influencing of the profession open to researchers who are several steps removed from day-to-day practice, and perhaps helps to contribute to the lack of fit between theory and practice (Stubbs, 1989). The practice and dissemination of practitioner research has implications for the practice of individual educators as well as offering the possibility of impacting the larger field of educational theory and practice.

The examples in this chapter illustrate a wide range of current practitioner research. Richards' (1989) research will resonate for many practitioners: What do I do with this class when it looks like *nothing* I do is effective? While initally investigating her own classroom practices, Richards crosses hierarchical lines and invites her students to be coinvestigators in discovering what might help them become more successful students. Russell (1992) and SooHoo (1991) provide illustrations of the potential for practitioner research to broaden into empowering practice. In Russell's case, other professionals became involved in the process and eventually spoke out on a district level. SooHoo, by including her students in the research process as coinvestigators, eventually helped create space for the students to become change agents.

Ballenger's (1993) work is a striking example of the power of the insider's lens brought to bear on research data. Only through her tacit knowledge of the children's relationships could Ballenger have come to the insights that allowed her to push the edges theoretically.

The examples from the Educators' Forum (Evans, 1989; Stubbs, 1989) as well as the principals' group (Christman et al., in press) demonstrate the use of the group process to support the conceptualization and implementation of research. Both groups function as sounding boards, providing the opportunity for professional dialogue, which is often difficult to build into the school day.

Methodologies in these studies vary. A number of the researchers (Ballenger, 1993, Christman et al., in press; Richards, 1989) utilize journal writing as a way to capture their day-to-day reflections and encounters; SooHoo (1991) asked her students to record meaningful learning experiences in a journal notebook and through photography and drawing. The principals' group (Christman et al., in press) used journals as a way to bring the reality of their school days and decision making to the group as a whole.

A number of the researchers (Christman et al., in press; Evans, 1989; Russell, 1992; Stubbs, 1989) relied on relationships with colleagues as part of the research process, "critical friends" with whom they could have sustained dialogues regarding their findings and methodologies. Both Richards (1989) and SooHoo (1991) moved students into the roles of collaborators in their research processes.

Observations, whether of their own classroom environment and student interactions with materials (Ballenger, 1993; Russell, 1992) or the shadowing of students as they went through their school day (Richards, 1989; SooHoo, 1991), were used to contextualize and understand the students' experiences of the school day. Audiotaping class activities and transcribing the tapes for analysis (Ballenger, 1993; Richards, 1989) were used in a similar way; teachers seemed to see taping as a way to capture the unfolding of the day-to-day educational process and to be able to analyze it later. These and other methodologies for practitioner research are discussed in depth in Chapter 5.

These examples of practitioner research touch on a range of possibilities. There are examples of university-school collaborations; research across authority lines such as students and teachers; research as part of professional development; and seasoned teachers studying their own classrooms, exploring the theoretical implications of their studies. The hope is that research possibilities pertinent to the reader's own practice site will begin to crystallize.

Research in the Classroom:
Monica Richards and the "Bums" of 8H

Classroom research often builds on the informal observing and questioning that teachers are already doing; ongoing quandaries about a practice question lead teachers to systematize the observation. Classroom research can be a way to document what "works" or a way to see if the teacher's "walk and talk" match. A teacher may be concerned about gender equity issues and the classroom may or may not match that concern. Classroom research is a way to bring intention to a conscious level of observation, to affirm or improve practice, to systematize problem solving, or to support a teacher taking on a new task.

In her narrative account of the "bums" of 8H, Richards (1989), a middle school language arts teacher, sets the scene for her research by letting the reader in on what motivated her to undertake her study in the first place:

> Every year I ask myself the same question, "How am I going to motivate a group of students who do not want to learn?" I employ many strategies, trying a new one or two every now and then, but none has ever been so effective that other students came knocking at my door for the "answer."
>
> In the past I had relied on suggestions by published researchers and educators or techniques recommended by my colleagues, but nothing came close to affecting my sixth period class, the self-styled "bums" from 8H. (p. 65)

Motivated by the kind of desperation that can occur when teachers are faced with a class where "nothing works," Richards moved

from a reliance on outside experts for answers to the idea of studying her own classroom. She broadened her original question about
how to motivate students who do not want to learn to include questions related to teacher behavior:

> What behavior must I exhibit/model to elicit an interested
> response at the onset of the class; how can I maintain that
> interest; and finally how can I get students to self-initiate
> verbal or written performance? What mode of interaction
> best facilitates motivation to achieve objectives? And what
> is it that occurs in highly motivational situations? I wanted
> to determine what environmental factors in the classroom
> might influence motivation, and what types of rewards are
> effective. (Richards, 1989, p. 66)

Richards used a methodology that included a daily journal; she
had previously intentionally left the "bums" of 8H out of her journal
"because the thoughts and words to describe what had happened
in 50 minutes with them were so horrendous that I could not bring
myself to write about them" (1989, p. 66). She also used tape recordings of class activities and student interviews and questionnaires.
To launch her study, she shadowed 8H as it proceeded through its
day, and although she was not surprised by what she saw, the
cumulative impact of her observations was staggering. Here was a
group making its way through the school day with little success or
affirmation of the learning process; the "bums" of 8H were obviously used to failure.

In what she terms "beginning again" with the group, Richards
read the students her research proposal, enlisting their help to communicate with her and to work together on the research process:

> I began reading my proposal for research to them. They all
> listened attentively. Even George, who usually cannot resist
> laying his head down for a short snooze, remained alert. "If
> we agree to work together, you will have to communicate
> with me." They all agreed to do so.
> I had no idea 8H could be so serious, so understanding.
> Reading my proposal had been the first step in working

together. I knew my perceptions of them were accurate, and they knew how I really felt about them and their neglect of the learning process. (Richards, 1989, p. 70)

By inviting her students into the problem-solving process, and by proposing to look at the impact of teacher behaviors as well as those of the students, Richards forged a partnership with her students that made for an exciting study.

Crossing the hierarchical lines that separate students and teachers is risky business, but in taking chances herself and being vulnerable to the students by asking for feedback, Richards invited the honest communication that was crucial to the study. She also invited her students into a reflective process that helped them demystify their own lack of success in the educational arena. This mutual vulnerability and reflexivity, with implications for change on the part of both the teacher and the students, set the stage for all to strategize together on what might best help them improve the learning process.

Richards (1989) began to try some interventions in her classroom; in her journal, she writes about an experiment in sending notes home to parents and the risks she felt in trying this:

About seven people had completed their homework. They read their compositions aloud. As I praised each one, I handed them a positive note to take home to their parents rewarding their good work in Language Arts today. Norman was especially happy about his. Proudly he showed it to the person in front of him—comparing notes possibly. Or was he laughing, making fun of it? This was my fear. Is Norman (and others like him in 8H) too cool, too macho to get a positive note from the teacher? I'll talk to them about this tomorrow. (p. 69)

Searching for other positive motivators for her class, Richards mounted a motivational bulletin board, with a horse on a race track, illustrating the progress the class was making in attendance, homework, and participation. She also devised a list of extrinsic motivators and tried to prioritize them in the way she thought her students would; for example, number 1 on her list was a bonus point system.

In keeping with the spirit of partnership in the problem-solving process, she shared the list with the class and asked the class to prioritize it as well. Richards (1989) writes about their process and her
own as she gained new information about the class:

> I discussed the priority of items on the checklist. I had as-
> sumed the number one item would be a bonus point system
> where the class earning the most bonus points in one six
> week period would choose their own reward. 8H rated it
> number ten, and after a little discussion decided it didn't
> even need to be on the list. They rated teaching resources
> number one. How wrong I was about them! I was also wrong
> about the positive notes home. I shared my fear about them
> being too "cool" for a positive note. Norman, Scott and
> Dawn all said that's not true. They said they took their notes
> home and showed them. Norman was serious. Dawn and
> Kim rated them especially high on their list—about second,
> with verbal praise a close third. . . .
>
> I was not only working with 8H to reorganize each
> strategy and develop classroom incentives, but I was valu-
> ing their ideas. They cooperated fully, taking the activity
> seriously. Everyone contributed ideas. . . .
>
> Clearly, I had wasted many days assuming 8H was inca-
> pable of deep reasoning. I was guilty of letting their outer
> appearance and low academic ability sway my attitude. I
> had underestimated them; I found that they were capable
> of mature thoughts. I soon came to realize that they not only
> needed but also appreciated a teacher who was knowledge-
> able and caring. (p. 71)

At the same time, Richards was allowing her own problem
solving to be informed through her reading of the literature on
motivation; she was then able to base her own proposed behavioral
changes on work that had been done in the area. For example, in
reading Maslow's hierarchy of human needs, Richards realized that
her students' need for warmth and acceptance had priority over
their need for achievement. In reflecting on the implications of this
for her as a teacher, she realized that "if I want my students to be

motivated to achieve, I must care for them as persons" (Richards, 1989, p. 72).

In addition, Richards allowed her reading to help frame her next intervention in the classroom; in this case, she worked on a 2-week unit with the students based on her reading of Bragstad and Stumpf (1982). She reflects that it

> helped clarify and put into perspective my focus on moti-vating students who do not want to learn. It also provided a framework, a definition, and an organizational pattern for discussing motivation and study skills on a more personal level. I not only wanted to get in touch with 8H, I wanted 8H to get in touch with themselves. (Richards, 1989, p. 72)

In writing about the positive results of the unit, Richards illus-trates that she gained insight into her own behaviors and that the students were able to identify some of the things inhibiting their own motivation, as well as strategize some possible interventions. In thinking about how well the unit had gone and the high level of student participation, Richards (1989) observes that the positive stu-dent behavior was due in part to the content of the lesson, but also due to the change in teacher behavior:

> I expected everyone to be successful and productive. They had vowed to communicate and work together with me. We had common expectations.
>
> In a tape-recorded session of 8H discussing a previous day's work, I discovered that retention was excellent. I asked them to restate, in order, their four largest inhibitors of motivation. These were (a) ". . . comparing me with another student in class," (b) "Picking out a certain group of students as pets," (c) "Lack of trust in students," and (d) "A teacher always 'cuts you down.' "
>
> A positive dimension of dealing with these inhibitors or "coping" devices were then restated: (a) get advice from a counselor, (b) talk privately with the individual with whom you have a conflict, (c) students' actions speak louder than words, and (d) have a cooperative attitude. (p. 73)

Documenting many positive changes in the day-to-day interaction and learning in her class, Richards and the class looked forward to report card day. In the unit study on motivation, students had voted that getting good grades was the first source of motivation. (Second to this, in the students' perception, was having parents care, followed by having a bright, caring teacher.) In Richards' own class, only 4 students out of 26 had lower grades than in the last marking period. In looking at their grades overall though, 5 students' grades were up, 9 students maintained their previous performance, and 12 students had grades that were lower. Richards (1989) writes:

> I was not pleased with the results. When asked why so many grades dropped or remained the same, the students placed the blame on the teachers for the most part. Remarks like "He don't like us," or "She doesn't know how to teach. All she does is pass out worksheets," had been said before and were now being repeated. (p. 75)

Trying to understand why, when the students had put so much emphasis on getting good grades, there was not more improvement in this area, Richards, in keeping with the spirit of the research, asked herself questions about behaviors of both students and teachers. She wondered whether the other teachers accepted the students as they were. Had they tried to find out where the students were? How did they grade? She wondered whether the students had fulfilled their end of the obligations. While puzzling over these issues in the larger realm of the students' experience in school, she was able to identify why things had improved in her own classroom:

> I can, however, explain why the students' grades in my classroom improved in four weeks. We had a common understanding that getting good grades was important; we were interested in the content of the lesson; we valued each other's ideas; we were working and learning together. This interchange of teaching and learning was the most valuable lesson to be learned.
>
> I also believe that what will be remembered in the minds of the students of 8H will not be a letter grade received in a

class, but rather the memories of having experienced success and praise for achieving, regardless of how small the achievements.

I had been mistaken about the students' potential because of their appearance. Blanchard and Johnson (1982) state that it's easy for any of us to make this mistake. Spending time discussing self-image and attitudes had proven beneficial. Until we openly shared our feelings about each other, there was a vacancy in my learning and in their learning. (Richards, 1989, pp. 75-76)

Richards ends her study with an increased awareness of her role as a teacher, as well a greater sense of her students and what motivates them. She also got the results she was looking for, that is, a class that performed at a higher level, as measured in their grades.

Although "ending" her research on this note, it seems that, considering the spirals of action research, Richards is well poised to begin the next round of questions, perhaps in a broader realm; she could pursue answers to some of her own queries as to why the students did not perform better in other classes. One suspects, based on Richards' research, that the necessary ingredients involve not only increasing the motivation of the students but also increasing reflexivity on the part of teachers and students as to what they contribute to the dynamic of failure. If Richards were to continue the research spiral, perhaps she would have the opportunity to share her own learning and classroom results in a larger arena, working with other educators in her school. This kind of dissemination of her research could have an impact beyond her classroom in the larger environment of the school, potentially creating a new context for learning for the "bums" of 8H.

Developing Teacher Voice: Robyn Russell

Russell's (1992) account of her practitioner research has as its starting point her own struggle with silence and voice; it grows to encompass an analysis of many layers of her school and larger professional issues in education. Russell's work is an example of how one individual's reflections and questions can become a powerful catalyst for the development of a multilevel approach to intervention in a school. In this summary of her work, we trace the development of Russell's research from her individual reflections to her institutional analysis. The research process helps Russell find her own voice and, as the research proceeds, she increasingly finds ways to use it.

A teacher in the Utah public school system, Russell was a participant in a graduate program, known as the Educative Research Project, offered through the University of Utah; the program works to explicitly challenge the hierarchical differences between teachers and academics (Gitlin et al., 1992). Believing such hierarchy silences teachers' voices and their input into educational reform, participants from the university and teaching communities work together to broaden the base on which such expertise is based. Linking understanding of the educational world with their ability to act in it, participants are encouraged to reflect on, examine, and remake schooling (Gitlin et al., 1992).

In her initial self-reflection, Russell contextualizes the ways that women are silenced in current society, linking that observation to her choice of the teaching profession; looking at the profession historically, she discovers that teachers have rarely had an active voice in educational theory and research.

As a master's degree student, Russell writes an account of her school's history that moves her into an analysis of the ways that school structures silence teachers. She analyzes the architecture of her classroom, the mandated curriculum, and the required textbooks, and juxtaposes these observations with the readings she was doing as part of the graduate program. Russell (1992) writes:

> These readings, including the works of Sarason (1971) and Jackson (1968), released me from the guilt of what I could not change, and gave me permission to change all I could. I gained confidence in my teaching. I began to speak out and not hide behind my "closed classroom door." This signified a major shift in my relation to the system. (pp. 91-92)

As part of her graduate program, Russell was paired with another teacher for ongoing dialogue, described as the Horizontal Evaluation Method. They were to analyze collaboratively the relationship between their teaching intentions and their practices, identifying the mismatches or thinking through why they wanted to achieve a particular end (Gitlin et al., 1992, p. 52). In this process, Russell came to the realization that teachers in general do not have a voice in educational reform; she observed that school structures, such as the teaching schedule, teacher isolation, and the historical feminization of teaching contributed to this silence. At the same time, Russell (1992) was observing a change in herself and formulating her research question.

> The simple act of talking about these issues began to change my professional life. I was beginning to gain a sense of empowerment. . . . These changes in my perception of the teacher role caused me to look at how others could also benefit from dialogue. A recurrent question began to appear in my thoughts and writing. How might our school, or even our profession, change if discussion and reflection were made available and encouraged? (p. 93)

This linking of her own experiences to the teaching profession in general, the larger institutional context, and the experiences of other teachers, led Russell to look for a way to establish a consistent block of time in her school for conducting dialogue among teachers about educational issues. She reasoned that if teachers could have time to talk among themselves, they might become more willing to express their ideas in a wider forum. Drawing on her own experience, having learned to express her thoughts as her trust with her dialogue partner grew, Russell (1992) hypothesized that the same would be true for teachers if they were offered a safe place to discuss their ideas:

> Somehow, I felt that the development of teacher voice was a key to membership in the historically exclusive club of educational decision making. Without a firm concept of what exactly I wanted to express, change or become empowered to do, I leaped into my research. All I knew with any certainty was that I wanted us to start talking to each other. (pp. 93-94)

She adds:

> I saw it as one possible avenue toward the restructuring of
> the educational hierarchy, of making some impact on the
> invisibility and silence that Thorne (1984) argues is an in-
> herent part of a gendered profession. . . . I yearned for new
> ways of making myself visible and heard, while bringing
> with me a chorus of other teachers. (Russell, 1992, p. 94)

Moving from a personal realm, her own struggles with being
silenced and working to find her voice, Russell began to contextualize
her own concerns and became aware of the larger forces that col-
luded not only to keep her silenced but her professional peers as
well. This kind of linking led to a different design for possible intervention; it was a move from the privatizing of a problem or issue
(i.e., "this is my struggle") to "this is my issue but many teachers
struggle in this way because of the design of educational institutions." The design of Russell's research moved her to intervene in a
way that might encourage teacher voice, with the larger agenda of
impacting educational theory and reform. Russell designed her research with the goal of restructuring the educational hierarchy and
affecting silencing.

She first surveyed the other teachers in her building regarding
their attitudes about professional dialogue on educational issues;
she asked how many would be interested in dialogue sessions,
should they be offered. Based on this information gathering, which
indicated a positive interest in the opportunity to talk with other
teachers, Russell organized voluntary teacher dialogue sessions, open
to any faculty in the school. The research continued over a period of
2 years, during which time Russell reflected on and made changes
in the process of teachers conversing together.

Russell and her partner in Horizontal Evaluation continued to
meet during this time, providing a second source of data. They met
following each of the teacher dialogue sessions "to compare the
intentions of the meetings with the realities of what actually transpired" (Russell, 1992, p. 95). The pair explored Russell's assumptions
about each meeting and planned for the next one. Russell analyzed

transcripts of each meeting with her partner to ascertain how the process of Horizontal Evaluation was influencing the dialogue sessions.

In writing about her 2 years of research, Russell explores themes that reflect her own questions. For example, she asks how much to structure and lead the dialogue groups, how to move them from "Robyn's meetings" to one of shared ownership. She reflects on themes that are common to many educational settings, such as how to create time in busy teachers' schedules for the dialogue groups or how to obtain compensation for the extra time if the groups are held outside of the regular school day. She puzzles over how to enlist administrative support and sanction. Interventions designed to solve some of the issues that arose then could vary from a reflection on her particular roles and changing her style of leadership in the meetings to working to convince administrators that allowing time for teacher-generated dialogue could result in positive results for education.

In the second year of the research, the teachers named their meetings Professional Dialogue Sessions (PDS), worked out a regular schedule to meet the third Friday of each month for lunch, and generated a list of topics to be discussed during the school year. Finding a collective voice, the PDS group decided to work on a specific project; they proposed a computer lab for the school despite the refusal of an earlier request by the administration. This type of empowered effort among teachers had been previously unheard of in the school; Russell attributed it to the organizational power of the dialogue group.

As is often the case in the life of researchers, intentional actions coincided with serendipitous events; in this case, the school district offered the possibility of piloting one of three computer systems. Members of the PDS became part of a larger computer committee asked to investigate and decide on a computer system; the committee was given a weekend to decide which one they wanted and were to recommend it at a faculty meeting the following Monday. Committee members, feeling that it was a mistake to make such a costly decision with so little time to investigate the options, reported that view to the larger faculty meeting:

Our faculty meeting became a forum for discussing the assumptions behind the administration's practice of giving us choice among limited options, and very little time for making informed, well-investigated decisions. The PDS group that had decided to present a proposal to the faculty for a computer lab recommended the rejection of the option to pilot any of the three systems on the premise that the district's procedure of limiting our choices was not a choice. The faculty enthusiastically approved. . . . Our faculty recognized and examined common parameters to the educational choice usually given teachers, such as choosing between a limited number of alternatives, and found them unacceptable. (Russell, 1992, p. 108)

The PDS group invited the district superintendent to its next group meeting; he accepted the invitation, which resulted in a working session. As often happens when dialogue is opened up, new information was gathered and perceptions were changed; the distribution of power was rearranged as teachers empowered through dialogue became a collective force, working together toward an agreed-upon end.

Reflecting on her 2 years of research, Russell was able to document changes occurring in herself, the teachers, and the administration. The Professional Dialogue Sessions continued in the next school year. Russell (1992) conceptualizes the next step in this process of uncovering and encouraging voice:

The personal and professional ramifications of this study expand in all directions for me as I see the broader implications of dialogue and educational empowerment. Parents and students have been even more discouraged from speaking than teachers. Eventually, I must find ways to include their voices as well. My hope is that I can encourage my students' voices while providing them with a receptive audience. This is what I have wished for myself. My personal journey to develop my teacher voice has taken me further down the path to the doors of more partners in silence than I imagined to be possible. (p. 115)

Students as Coinvestigators
in the Research Process: Suzanne SooHoo

Just as teachers struggle to find voice, the views of students have rarely been solicited to inform educational practice and reform. Interested in exploring what makes up meaningful learning experiences for middle school students, SooHoo (1991) invited students to become her coinvestigators. Not originally conceptualized as action research, her study led to the conclusion that when student voice is solicited, it is an empowering process that lends itself to action; for SooHoo, coming into the site as a doctoral student from a nearby university, this presented tricky waters to navigate as she worked to honor her relationships with the students and the school involved.

Wondering how students understand their learning processes and their learning environment, SooHoo originally thought to investigate what students consider meaningful learning experiences. Her work with the student coinvestigators soon led them to reconceptualize the questions:

> It was understood from the beginning that they would help me identify meaningful learning experiences. . . . They would be active in data collection, analysis, and research findings. They were more than research subjects. They were key informants who collaborated with me throughout the research. By empowering them with this responsibility, we gave voice to a group who historically have not been systematically included in the research community.
>
> Over the course of the study, the students became more than key informants. Unintentionally they evolved into agents of change. This was the result of refinement of the research question. Because students could not tell me what meaningful learning experiences were, but they could tell me what they were not, I redefined the research question to "what are the obstacles to learning?" (SooHoo, 1991, pp. 6-7)

Mixed with SooHoo's own data gathering—shadowing students and interviewing them individually and in groups—were techniques for data gathering by the students. Students were given cameras to photograph "meaningful learning experiences" both in and out of the classroom. SooHoo also distributed notebooks for students to keep a learning journal, documenting classroom activities period by period. In addition, SooHoo asked students to draw "pictures of what they thought happened in their minds when learning transpired" (SooHoo, 1991, p. 4). They then used these sources of data in their biweekly, coresearcher meetings as a basis for conversation and analysis; SooHoo's observations were shared at the meetings as well, allowing students to clarify misconceptions or volunteer further data.

SooHoo discovered that the process of being involved in the research process and identification of the barriers students saw in their learning environment gave the students a sense of empowerment. As she states, "Student voice evolved" (1991, p. 7). With it came a sense of wanting to work for change in the learning environment, moving the research into the realms of action. SooHoo documents this progression and what was going through her own mind at this time:

Drawing strength from each other, the co-researchers expressed a compelling need to actively reshape their learning conditions. Discussions about alternatives and reform infused the dialogue and eventually prompted the development of an action plan, a plan to move beyond our meeting room and to take these concerns to someone who could do something about them. Virtually every attempt made by me to restrict the scope of the research would snap back to a growing conviction which could actively address the problems at the school.

At this point, I remember reflecting about the fate of my research. What had happened? What were my responsibilities to the students, teachers, and principal of this school? The students were pushing for a political agenda. The teachers and principal had no inkling this project could take this course. Did my research responsibilities conflict with a moral responsibility to support the students? Were the students serious about bringing attention to their findings? (SooHoo, 1991, pp. 7-8)

Adding to her queries and feelings of discomfort was the knowledge that students were convening their own meetings, outside of the regular research meetings. Empowerment and collaboration in this case meant that the students rightfully felt they, as well as SooHoo, "owned" the process and could strategize as to action to be taken; although this makes sense from an empowerment model, it raises the anxiety and confusion level of the adults who feel they must answer for a research process no longer solely under their control.

Working to build partnerships, SooHoo approached both the students and the school's principal about meeting together to discuss the students' findings and concerns. Both readily agreed; SooHoo identifies this as a turning point in the research: "this is where my research takes on the dimension of action research. The identification of barriers to learning resisted the confines of an academic exercise and propelled itself into action" (SooHoo, 1991, p. 9).

The barriers identified in their findings included classroom and school practices as well as relationship issues between teachers and students. For example, in the category "the rhythm of care and connection," students identified

> teachers who had "an attitude" as those who didn't care about students and who frequently prevented students from caring or connecting with each other. Teachers with "an attitude" denied students' connections with their homes, cultural heritage, friends, and subjective ways of knowing. Students reasoned they could not learn from teachers who did not care. Teachers reasoned these needs are outside of the purview of (the) classroom. Teachers saw approximately one hundred twenty students each day. There was no time to really get to know the students, therefore they became victims of the students' label, "teacher with an attitude." (Soo Hoo, 1991, pp. 12-13)

Students, in the past, had coped with learning barriers such as these in various ways: "ignoring" teachers, becoming "invisible," going underground, "splitting" their personalities to encompass classroom and "real" personas (SooHoo, 1991, p. 19). The meetings of the coresearchers helped the students conceptualize how they might become united activists on their own behalf, as well as for the student body at large, rather than relying on solely individual "solutions."

Prepared first by SooHoo, teachers and students met to discuss the implications of the findings. One teacher reports her feelings after the first meeting together:

> They, "the students," weakened us with goodies they pro- vided, and we, "the teachers," were human in the eyes of the students for the first time. Time had passed so quickly, we all agreed another meeting would be necessary and fruitful to begin the process of hearing these student voices and try to apply their suggestions to our classes. The ball was rolling. We want to establish a closer student-teacher rela- tionship and jointly formulate strategies for student partici- pation in crating positive learning experiences. (SooHoo, 1991, pp. 21-22)

Students met next with the principal, and with her support two new ad hoc principal advisory groups were formed, with the under- standing that they would incorporate coresearcher involvement and input. One advisory group looked at the physical education expec- tations in the school, considered "militaristic" by the students; the other advisory group updated and revised the disciplinary policy. Later in the year, the coresearchers worked with their teachers to construct thematic curricula during a 3-day planning session.

SooHoo documents that there were other spin-off effects from the research; the principal and at least one teacher launched research inquiries of their own. The teacher began a reflective journal in response to student concerns, sharing her thoughts with SooHoo (1991), who acted in the role of critical friend:

> I acted as a resource by providing an independent view- point when she requested it. She consistently sought oppor- tunities to intellectually engage in issues about her classroom. Perhaps this format is the authentic link between universities and schools. (p. 25)

The principal studied staff development activities, looking at which were most effective in light of the students' findings. From the principal's view, there was a new awareness that students were an influential source of input where decision making in the school was concerned: "Her previous commitment to cultivate a school climate of collegiality, now compelled her to invite students to the decision making table" (SooHoo, 1991, p. 28).

For the students, being involved in the research process had multiple benefits. They supported each other, sharing stories and experiences; they were empowered to critique, challenge, and suggest alternatives, developing individual and collective reforms. SooHoo describes the students as virtual "mutes" at the beginning of the research; they eventually became aware of their tacit knowledge and became comfortable making that knowledge public.In describing the voyage of one particular student, SooHoo (1991) writes:

> The transformation of one particular student, Juan, was particularly significant. As mentioned before, he was the Hispanic male who was Mr. Soc. in the halls and Mr. Placid in the classrooms. He reinforced this duality by referring to himself as "John" in the classrooms, and "Juan" outside the classroom. Juan was confident and socially connected to his peers, John was withdrawn and indifferent to classroom activities. At "the meeting" with the teachers, Juan was expressive and self-assured as he boldly pointed out instances of Hispanic discrimination, a side the teachers hadn't seen before. They commented, "we saw John take a position, be a leader, dominate the discussion." At the end of the year, Juan, previously a "C" student graduated with all "A's" and "B's" and was voted most improved student of the year by his teachers. (p. 27)

Although not originally conceptualized as an action research project, and not constructed as a vehicle for change, SooHoo's willingness to honor the students' voices and to allow the research to develop in ways that she had not originally anticipated meant that the people in the institution were touched in very real ways. She created a safe place for students to find their voices and then helped pave a way

for them to express their thoughts in a larger arena. The students'
roles as coresearchers inspired changes in themselves and in their
learning environment.

Expanding Theory Through
Teacher Research: Cindy Ballenger

Ballenger (1993), a preschool teacher in a Haitian community in
Dorchester, MA, studied how the preschoolers in her classroom
approached learning about print and found herself identifying in-
adequacies in models of literacy learning. Her observations and
reflections of her students did not seem to "fit" with current explanations of ways students acquire literacy knowledge; her research
pushes us to consider "other ways of knowing." Hers is an example
of practitioner research that informed and expanded the existing
theory base.

In this bilingual preschool, which serves mainly the children of
Haitian immigrants, Ballenger, the staff at the community center,
and the children fluidly move between Haitian Creole and English.
Ballenger's teacher's aide was not rehired when budget cuts forced
a reallocation of money. Ballenger (1993) writes of the impact of not
having an aide:

> Without an aide, I found myself in the position of observer
> much more than I otherwise would have been. I became
> increasingly aware of the extraordinary ability these chil-
> dren had to take care of themselves. They took each other
> to the bathroom, helped each other with jackets, knew when
> it was the right moment to invite an angry child back into
> the group, even reprimanded each other when it was appro-
> priate. I taught these children—but I also sat back more
> than usual and watched them run their own small community.
> (p. 10)

Through the processes of writing journals and transcribing audio-
tapes of her classroom, Ballenger documented her students' unique
approach to literacy learning. She began to define a "shadow curricu-

lum," the students' curriculum, that supported their learning, almost in spite of the intrusion of the teacher's curriculum.

Reflecting on her own curriculum for the preschool classroom, Ballenger saw as part of her job exposing children to print and letting them experience its many functions; she expected them to generate hypotheses about what print is and is not:

> I expect that these hypotheses will be continually reanalyzed and corrected by the child in light of his/her continuing experience with print. I see my job as making sure that the experiences are there. I do this both by explicit teaching of facts ("No, that is not your name yet. You need a Y at the end."); by drawing their attention to contradictions in their theories ("Only girls can have S's? What about Steve? And here's an S in Rubenson."); and by doing lots of reading and writing. At the same time I really value the kind of thinking that goes on in these hypotheses, right or wrong. I see it as logical thinking, as analysis. (Ballenger, 1993, p. 11)

Ballenger soon realized that the children did not experience print in the same way; her journals and transcriptions reveal the children's meaning-making of letters, what Ballenger eventually called their "shadow curriculum, events which involved print, but which were outside my plans and expectations" (Ballenger, 1993, p. 13). Following are some of her examples of this.

Note 1: Marc calls Sora to show her whenever he finds an S among the letters. "Sora, your S." She obediently goes to him each time she is called and looks at the letter he is indicating, then returns to whatever she is playing.

Note 2: Mackson spells his name: M for Mackson, A for Andy, C for Carl, K for Kellie, S for Sora—and then he stops; he cannot go further since he knows no one whose name begins with O or with N.

Note 3: Tiny Tatie, not yet three years old, never says a word and never comes to circle where we read the names and talk a little about letters. I am amazed to discover that she has been walking around all morning with two fingers in the shape of a T. When asked what she's doing, she says, "it's me," and continues silently to parade her T around the classroom. . . .

Note 6: Giles is just four years old. He had learned to write his whole name. This day Giles is making his G, announcing it as he goes. "Cindy, I make my G." He cuts the paper on which he has written, carefully avoiding the G, and parades around the classroom saying, "I no cut my G." He repeats the process, making more G's and not cutting them many times this morning, each time announcing to me and the world, "Cindy, I no cut my G." Finally I find myself saying to him, "No, Giles, I see. You take good care of your G" as if he were carrying a doll around instead of a letter. Giles later appears with a P for Paul and an R for Rafi, his two best buddies. He doesn't cut them either, as he tells us all. Next he makes an S for Steven, whom he does not like. "I cut Steven's S," he announces in a dire tone.

Working to understand this shadow curriculum, Ballenger moves from looking at individual children's responses to print to a more general view. In making meaning of observations of individuals, Ballenger writes:

Marc: What is Marc doing in field note 1? He and Sora are playing together. The activity is keeping track of Sora's S's. There is another girl whose name begins with S, as Marc well knows, but she and Marc are not particularly close, so it is Sora that he calls to him each time he can find an S. Print is part of being friends with Sora, and being friends with Sora is a way to use print.

Mackson: The way Mackson spells, using everyone's name, becomes typical for the classroom. All the children who can, identify the letters of their name in this way. I initially try to break them of the habit, assuming that they have the mistaken impression that you can own letters, that your letter is yours and yours alone. I am therefore always telling them that it is not really Tatie's T, for example. Other children and other words also have T's. We always observe when more than one child's name begins with the same letter. The children accept what I say and learn that turtle begins with T and that stop has a T. However, nothing breaks them of this way of spelling, and finally I become charmed by it myself. Again, print and friendship proceed together.

Tatie: Tatie, the youngest in the class, tries to keep all the T's—coloring papers, magnetic T's, and cut-out letters—in her cubby. She knows that she shares T at least with Teo, another child in the classroom. She is a very silent child, although obviously aware. In note 4 Tatie has used the S and her T to greet, to make some sort of social connection with Sora's mother at a point where she is still not willing to talk.

Giles: Giles places his own letter on the public stage by announcing it and his care for it. He then includes his two friends in the circle of his care, and acts out his opposite feeling for another member of the group. He uses letters to comment upon his connections with, and feelings for, his friends. He is acting on a stage of his own creation when he cuts Steve's S. . . . Giles. . . . keeps repeating that he hasn't cut his G. He does not appear satisfied until I finally say, "Yes, Giles, I see. You take good care of your G." At that point he goes on to make other letters and act upon them. What is behind such persistence?

The final response is from a completely different area of a teacher's repertoire. "You take good care of your G" is the sort of response I make when children are playing in the house corner with babies. In my particular case, it is intended to be a comment on separation. It refers to the care that the child receives at home, and the ability s/he has to carry that care with him or her as s/he goes to school. Giles had moved us into the symbolic drama of everyday life. I was not consciously aware of this move. When I heard my response on the tape, I recognized it and its source, although I never decided consciously to respond to him in this way. Something in his tone must have prompted my response. Having received it, Giles went on to develop his drama. (Ballenger, 1993, pp. 15-16)

In moving to the offerings of theory to understand her children's creations with print, Ballenger finds them lacking. Generally seeing children's acquisition of print as a precursor to understanding the logic of reading and writing, the existing models seem to imply that children learn print when they are motivated by the acquisition of scientific or technical knowledge. Ballenger critiques these models as part of the world of "literalness"and states that "this model is not adequate for the approach taken by my children" (Ballenger, 1993, p. 17). She sees her children using print as representative of their social network, an observation that pushes existing theory. It is important to note that, without Ballenger's tacit knowledge of the existing relationships among her children, her meaning-making of what she was seeing and hearing could have taken her in extremely different directions; the framing of the data in relational terms pushed her toward theory questioning and expansion.

Group Process in Support
of Practitioner Research: The Principals' Group

Perhaps because practitioners do not necessarily find encouragement in their own school sites to see themselves as researchers, and perhaps because of the isolation many educators face in their day-to-day practice, the formation of wide-reaching groups outside of the school site for the support and feedback of reflective practitioners as researchers is highly appealing to many of us. For those who are currently the sole researchers in their sites, the groups act as a forum for research development and critical thinking about data gathered. Although many of us would prefer to be part of a site-based "community of inquiry" within our own schools, a group of educators outside our sites may be an alternate source of support and encouragement when the former is not available. As the following examples illustrate, there is room for much fruitful collaboration when practitioners isolated in roles at their own schools find and work with their counterparts in other sites.

The first example is drawn from the work of five female elementary and middle school principals and an educational ethnographer who are part of a principals' journal group (Christman et al., in press). The presentation of their journal writings for themselves and each other twice a month has become a catalyst for action in their individual work sites. Although each practices as a lone administrator during the work week, each has the benefit of the thoughts of others in similar positions during their meetings. Following the premises of action research, working through the spiral of problem posing, reflection, action, and observation, the journal group is a forum for the conceptualization of these steps.

The principals see the journal group as "feminist activity, good old fashioned consciousness raising, because naming and understanding our experience as the 'other,' women principals in a still male-dominated profession, is an acknowledged, central purpose" (Christman et al., in press, p. 22). They ask themselves, "Can we be feminist principals? Can we exercise the power and authority of our positions as principals within a context of connection to and care for the other?" (p. 22).

One of the principals in the group, Arlene Holtz, relates what she terms the one piece of her journal that stands out "as a marker, a turning point in my development as a principal" (Christman et al., in press, p. 9). The other participants in the group describe the part they have seen themselves play in her work: "We began as her audience, but . . . we transformed ourselves into co-investigators and conspirators" (p. 9).

The incident, which Holtz writes about in her journal, happened in the middle school in which she is the principal, a school desegregated by busing African American students. An African American female student, Takia, was brusquely brought to Holtz's office by one of the male teaching assistants who had caught her on the playground with a 6-inch knife. Holtz recorded the incident in her journal for her own reflection as well as for the group:

> Gingerly, I released the catch and pulled back the brass casing. A six inch blade, sharpened on both sides, emerged.
>
> *"She was carrying it open beside her thigh in the yard," he (the teaching assistant) said.*
>
> There were 350 kids playing outside at lunchtime and I shuddered at the thought of what she might have done with it.
>
> *"She threw it into her girlfriend's pocketbook when I tried to take it from her." He produced a small black shoulder bag, with*

the thin strap broken. "Her girlfriend wouldn't release the
bag, so I snapped it off her shoulder."

I shook my head knowing that would mean trouble down
the road.

"Then she jumped on me from behind and started pounding my
back."

With this Takia began an unintelligible outburst.

"I didn't tell you to talk," I snapped. "Shut up!" (pp. 9-10)

At this point in the story, Kneesha, the student who owned the
pocketbook, entered the office with one of the 7th grade teachers.

"She was innocent," the teacher said. "Takia threw the knife into
her bag."
"Did you let go of the bag when Mr. O. asked for it?" I asked.
"He didn't ask," she sobbed. "He just grabbed it."
"That's a lie!" Mr. O. shouted.
"Mr. O.," I said, "just put it in writing."

As I write this now I wonder what I was thinking as this
unfolded. I'm a principal, an educator. This was police work.
I have no stomach for it. For crying-out-loud my strengths
were supposedly language arts, curriculum, middle school
organization. This was as far from all of that as I could get.
(Christman et al., in press, p. 19)

The 7th grade teacher again reiterated that the student with the
pocketbook was innocent. "She's an honor roll student. She's very
upset." Holtz reflects, "Honor Roll carried substantial weight with
me. I looked at Kneesha with new eyes and saw a frightened child, not
a criminal. I realized she was afraid of me. Her fate lay in my hands"
(Christman et al., in press, p. 10).
    Eventually, Takia admits that Kneesha had nothing to do with
the incident, that she had indeed put the knife in Kneesha's pocket-

book. Extracting a promise from Holtz that she would not allow anything to happen to Kneesha, the student eventually confessed to bringing the knife to school for her own protection because some girls had been bothering her on the way home from school.

Holtz continues with the journal:

> I telephoned both girls' mothers and then the police. . . . Two white officers arrived in my office. Neither made eye contact with me. I called in Mr. O. and asked him to tell what happened. He spoke as I handed the officer the knife. The cop refused to take it.
>
> *"So what do you want?" the cop asked. "I guess we'll take both girls."*
> *"No," I said. Not both. Just one."*
> *He looked at me. "Look, we'll let J.A.D. sort it out."*
> *"No," I said. "You either take one, or no one."*
> *"You tryin' to tell me my business?"*
> *"No," I said. "I'm the principal and I'm reporting that we confiscated a knife from this student." I point to Takia. "She threw it into this girl's pocketbook. She had nothing to do with it." I sat beside Kneesha and put my arm around her tightly. "You can't take her. If you do, I'll withdraw everything."*
> *"I won't!" Mr. O. said. "My back hurts from the pounding I took."*
> *"All right, all right," the cop said. "Stand up," he said to Takia, "and put your hands behind you." As he snapped the handcuffs on her she began to cry.*
> *"I'm not hurting you," he said meanly. "This would hurt." He did something I couldn't see which made Takia arch her back. "I'll leave 'em loose, but don't fight me."*
> *Takia spoke. "I'm scared, Dr. Holtz. I'm scared. You didn't tell me it would be like this."*

Something inside me broke, some silenced emotion I had held in check. Finally, I saw Takia as a child who was frightened and somehow linked to me as her only support in a terrifying world. (Christman et al., in press, p. 12)

Later, after Takia had been led away by the police, Kneesha's mother arrived.

"I'm glad you're here," I told her.
Before I could speak further, she interrupted me. "What do you plan to do about this pocketbook?"
I looked at it. "I think it can be easily repaired," I said. "Mr. O.'s first concern was to get the knife out of harm's way."
"He could have asked politely."
"Well, I think he did ask her, but she clutched the bag and wouldn't give it to him."
"Then he could have gotten someone else to speak to her."
"There was an open knife in the pocketbook," I said. "He secured it for safety reasons."
"You can tell my lawyer that."
"What?"
"Oh, I intend to sue you."
"Me, what for?"
"Did you reprimand Mr. O.?"
"Reprimand him? No. Mr. O., I think, did his best. It was an unfortunate—"
"Oh, I'm sick of listening to you. Tell it to my lawyer. You have no appreciation for our children's feelings."

I felt slapped across the face. What was this whole day about?

"Tell your lawyer to call our lawyer," I said. "I don't talk to lawyers."

I resumed my walk around the school, but I no longer saw anything, except anger and frustration. Ironically my thoughts turned to Takia. I realized I felt worried about her. (Christman et al., in press, p. 13)

Holtz's journal is one of her central sources of data for the process-ing of her role as principal—through her own meaning-making as well as through the input of the group. As a beautifully written example of journal writing, it serves as her group's lens into her school situation; the group is not on site together, so in order to share knowledge of each other's work place, they depend on the data the journals offer for their meaning making. Bringing fresh eyes to what is a familiar setting for Holtz, the group made meaning of incidents in ways that were not immediately apparent to Holtz herself; in this example, the group introduced race as a factor in the dynamics of the exchange. Holtz first worked to make sense of the incident herself, reflecting on the turn of events and how she handled them. She used the process of journal writing to gain further insight into her job as principal. Reflecting on the incident, Holtz writes about what she sees as "the myths of the principalship":

> I entered the principalship with the idea that what mattered most was what happened inside classrooms. I was dedicated to improving the teaching/learning in our school. I considered all this other stuff as extraneous and unimportant. I saw the problems associated with discipline as roadblocks I had to negotiate in order to get on with the important work such as improving instruction. The events in this journal forced me to reconsider this attitude. By the end of the journal Takia really matters to me. I move from her punisher to her protector. I assume my rightful role of teacher who cares about what happens to her in the future. I entered the principalship with the mistaken notion that I could delegate this kind of work to someone else. I can't. I shouldn't. What happens to Takia is as important as what happens to the honor student. Each child matters. It all matters. (Christman et al., in press, pp. 13-14)

Holtz went on to reflect on her own role in the incident. She felt that while she encouraged Takia to get through the ordeal with a shred of dig- nity, the attitude and behavior of the police—one of contempt and meanness—made her feel that she did not do enough, that somehow she betrayed Takia as well. Holtz writes of how things ended with Kneesha:

I do manage to protect her only to be slapped in the face by her mother when she threatens to sue me. I ended the day on a very low note.

It was only in our journal group that I began to feel forgiveness for how I handled the matter. Holly (another principal in the group) said, "Arlene is trying to choose in the moment what is best for the children, and all in all, doing a good job, but still feeling so bad, so bitter, somehow off the mark. It reminds me of situational ethics. The importance of understanding the context, the situation, in order to understand the decisions we make." It is only in our group that I find acceptance and safety in which I can explore events such as those I described. (Christman et al., in press, p. 14)

The group members then pointed out the themes regarding race that they heard in the story; there was nothing in Holtz's previous reflections on the incident that indicated she thought about it in racial terms. Holtz writes:

After hearing me read this journal Mollie reread the end where Kneesha's mother tells me, "You have no appreciation for our children's feelings." Mollie said, "This is about race. I see race issues throughout this piece." Without waiting to hear a word of what happened she passes judgment on my actions because I am white and the children are black. Her reaction is the worst part of the day for me. (Christman et al., in press, pp. 14-15)

But Holtz moves from this point of pain and takes in the feedback of Mollie. She reflects, "Although I don't explicitly state it, there is a question in my mind about whether O., a white man, had to rip the strap to obtain Kneesha's pocketbook. Issues of race do run throughout the piece" (Christman et al., in press, p. 15).

What is important in this example is the function of the group in expanding Holtz's vision of her practice. Although Holtz did not initially name race as a factor in the incident, when group members named it for her, she acknowledged their truth. The group allowed for an honest reflection and acceptance of feedback because of the level of trust that they had built. In this way, the group mirrors the cycle of action research: they present their practice puzzles, they reflect together, those reflections potentially impact their practice, and then they continue to bring their observations to the group to begin the cycle again.

This journal group saw itself as creating a space "where we can examine and forgive within institutions that too often ignore and blame" (Christman et al., in press, p. 22). Members asked how to honor their sense of connection with the children and parents they deal with day to day and wondered whether "we can forgive ourselves when we miss the mark? So that we can wave to the experience and move on to more thoughtful, more purposeful practice" (p. 22). The sense of support and honesty in the group make possible that kind of growth.

A Research Seminar
for Teachers: The Educators' Forum

The Educators' Forum has as its goal the support of teachers as they carry out their research. Evans (1989) and Stubbs (1989), among others (see also Evans, Stubbs, Duckworth, & Davis, 1981; Evans, Stubbs, Frechette, Neely, & Warner, 1987; Frechette, 1987), have written about their involvement in this seminar for teachers. Voluntary in nature, the seminar is open to elementary and secondary teachers in both public and private schools in Boston and the surrounding suburban areas. At the time Evans and Stubbs were writing about the forum there were 14 members, all women, participating in the seminar; these women ranged from first-year teachers to a career teacher about to retire, and they represented elementary and secondary classrooms of regular students, and those "at risk." An administrator from a public school served as the seminar leader. None of the participants received university credit or payment for their involvement.

Based on the realization that few structures help teachers think deeply and clearly about their work, the forum was started in the fall of 1985. Teachers gathered together to meet for 2 hours biweekly during the school year. Each member was encouraged to choose an issue or concern directly related to her classroom practice and to carry out research on that topic. The other participants acted as a type of advisory board; at each meeting three to four members presented their work to the other members, who helped the presenter focus, define a question, select data collection procedures, and make sense of the results. In addition, participants were encouraged to write regularly—for themselves, to clarify their thinking and for their colleagues, to disseminate their findings through presentations or publications.

The original orientation of the forum was toward individual classroom research. In the past several years, teachers have designed and carried out projects that have been more far-ranging than that original orientation. For example, one special-needs teacher in an elementary school was concerned that each year there were several 1st grade students who failed. Wanting to provide a solid start for each child, she wondered how to achieve "zero failure" in 1st grade. She had each of the 1st grade teachers identify students who were at risk of failure and developed a reading and language arts program that supported these students before they experienced failure; the program was staffed by regular, special-needs, and remedial reading teachers as well as parent volunteers trained by the investigating teacher. The ongoing evaluation of the program showed a great deal of success, and the program continued beyond the 1-year experiment. The program is being considered for adoption throughout her school system.

The sounding board of the forum encourages individual members to devise and carry out their own research; individuals benefit from the collective thinking of the group. In addition, the forum itself is part of an action research project, being studied and refined as it is developed through the years:

> As we have developed and conducted the seminar, we have studied it as well. As a result, we are able to answer questions in this paper which we could not have answered when we began the Forum: Is a biweekly seminar sufficient support for teachers to enable them to conduct classroom investigations? Will teachers find classroom research interesting and rewarding? Will teachers overcome their awe of "Research"

and "Researchers" and gain enough confidence to write for research meetings and for publication? (Evans, 1989, p. 1)

The response to each of these questions seems to be a resounding "yes." The Educators' Forum moves our knowledge base of how to support educators interested in research and helps sustain the ongoing movement of educator inquiry while generating data.

Final Thoughts

A reason for compiling this chapter of examples is to convey the exciting and important work currently being done by practitioners in their education sites. The puzzles that form the basis for the initial research are often "personal," that is, educators wondering how to improve what it is educators do. The evolution of the research process often takes them beyond the bounds of their own classrooms and into broader realms of educational issues. Typically this broader involvement comes out of the spiral of action and intervention that flows from the researchers' data gathering and meaning-making.

As practitioners gain their voice, self-consciously observing and recording their day-to-day activities and using tacit knowledge to inform their data further, the implications for the field of education —from improving practice to rethinking research methodologies to expanding theory bases—are varied and exciting. The courage to follow the research process and take ongoing actions based on it is part of what is noteworthy here; it is also what can put practitioner research in the vanguard of educational change.

4

Empowerment
and Practitioner Research
An Example

To illustrate the research being done by practitioners at their own
sites, we offer the following lengthy case example of work being
done by Herr (see also Herr & Anderson, 1993) in her school setting.
Because the research is still in progress, this chapter should be read
as a work in process.

Getting Started

For the independent school I work in, April is often a make or
break time; students not doing well academically or who are having
major difficulties with the discipline system run the risk of not being
re-enrolled for the next school year. The students in the school are
all of high ability academically, having had to gain entrance to the
school through a difficult admissions process. Several years ago, I
mentally went through the list of students that I, as a middle school
counselor and teacher, had worked with intensely. Many were stu-

dents of color or of socioeconomic backgrounds lower than the norm for the school; some were students that the school had recruited as part of a goal to diversify the school racially and socioeconomically. I concluded that a fair number of them were hanging by a thread; the end of the school year could find some of them gone or it could bring the possibility of another year of struggle. Either way, I was discouraged, feeling that somehow I should know how to do all of this better, how to help them be more successful.

I found myself mentally rehearsing the stories the students told me of their day-to-day experiences in the school. Although it once had a wealthy, all-male, student body that was predominately Anglo, the school had actively worked in the past few years to diversify its student population. Now coed, it boasted one of the larger populations of students of color in independent schools. Through a solid endowment, the school was able to offer a great deal of financial aid to provide opportunities to talented students who could not afford the tuition. But while this active recruitment and financial aid made it possible for a diversity of students to come to the school, it was not enough to retain them. Particularly at risk were the students of color who were also of a lower socioeconomic background; the combination of risk factors seemed to put them in particular jeopardy. I was also aware that, despite working vehemently on their behalf, my own intervention as a school counselor and teacher was not enough. I was concerned about what appeared to be a growing sentiment among some at the school: a blaming of the students if they did not appear to be able to "take advantage of the educational opportunity being offered them" through admittance to the school. There was also a quiet groundswell questioning whether the school had lowered its admission standards in admitting these students in the first place.

I was looking for ways to improve my own practice, but I was also aware that the stories that I was hearing in the confines of my counseling office had broader implications as the school grappled with what it meant to be a truly diverse institution. I was looking for a way to bring the students' stories into the public domain, so that the institution could hear the same voices I heard in my counseling sessions and factor them into the change equation of the school. Ethically, I did not feel I could privatize their stories, or pretend that the only site for intervention rested with the students themselves; I was trained in social work, and my framework suggested that the resolution to problems was in the interaction between the students and their school environment. I wanted to understand better the lack of fit between the students and the institution, and although I wanted to continue to work with the students, I wanted to understand the ways that we as an institution needed to grow as well.

It was out of this frustration that the "stories of students of color" research was born. Feeling vulnerable to blind spots in my status as an Anglo woman, I joined two other colleagues in the school to conceptualize the stories project. Working with a Hispanic administrator and an African American teacher, we agreed to attempt to raise the students' stories to a level of public awareness in the school. The African American teacher and I would do the interviewing.

One goal of this study was to broaden the definition of legitimate discourse in the school by explicitly asking students to reflect on and verbalize, in the interview process, their experiences as minority students in the school. The "grand tour" question was: "Tell me what it's like being a student of color here." The wording of the question was deliberate; through asking directly about their experiences as students of color, we were attempting to offer a "legitimating voice," that is, we were recognizing and expecting that their experiences were different from that of the majority. The goal was to convey an acknowledgment of the belief that there is power in the social construction and meaning attached to race and ethnicity (as well as gender, age, and sexual preference).

We ended the school year with a few interviews completed. I had asked a few middle school students whom I knew well to participate in the study; the teacher had targeted a few graduating seniors, wanting to get their reflections as students who had been in the school for a period of years and had, apparently, navigated the experience successfully. We had the taped interviews transcribed and then traded interview stories. We were buoyed by the richness of the stories that the students were sharing; a taste of listening to their experiences convinced us that we were on a path that had much to teach us. We committed to continuing the project into the next school year.

Now 3 years into the study, the focus of this chapter is on the issues presented for a researcher studying one's own site, particularly when the research critiques some of the institution's practices and when the research effort is part of an empowering process for the participants involved. What began as a fairly typical research interview study grew into more of a collaborative, action-oriented effort involving the students, my fellow research colleague, and me.

Although the interviews provided a wealth of information regarding the "lived experiences" of students of color in the school, just as important was the impact of the interview process itself on the students. In their research with adolescent girls, Brown and Gilligan (1992) discuss the power of placing girls in the position of being "experts" on their own lives, coupled with adults wanting to hear student voices and soliciting their stories. Rose (1990) suggests that one of the roles for the practitioner involved in empowering practice is the development of a dialogue with the client, assisting the client in expressing, elaborating, externalizing, and critically reflecting upon feelings and understandings of daily life events. As students named their reality in terms other than personal failure, that is, analyzed and critiqued the school environment in which they were expected to function, they sought ways to change the very composition of the institution. The research questioning served as a catalyst to begin the change effort.

The Process of Empowerment

My research colleague and I asked an African American male high school student to gather a small group of his friends for a group interview. He was a student I had known since his days as a 6th grader in the school; experiencing his own ups and downs through the years, he was a freshman when these interviews began. As a full-time teacher and a school counselor/teacher doing this research in our "spare" time, a group interview format was used for expediency as well as in the name of methodological experimentation. We hoped to gather a broader sample of stories than our individual interview format had yielded and to speed up the research process; we were also curious about the effect on the students of hearing each others' experiences in the same school. We wondered whether hearing each other would act as a catalyst in drawing out further reflections from the students. Our hunch was that students of color in our school rarely had the chance to trade stories, and we were curious as to what would evolve if such an opportunity were provided.

We were also interested in experimenting with joint interviewing. Previously, I had interviewed a student, for example an African American girl, then my colleague had interviewed the student; we both then reviewed the data to ascertain whether there were differences in the data when gathered by a female interviewer with a female interviewee and an African American interviewer with an African American. Our experiments with interview formats were leading us across racial and gender lines, and now from a one-on-one interview to a joint interview format with a group of students.

The original premise of the research was that my colleague and I would gather the students' stories and figure out a way to present their experiences to a larger audience in the school. Originally the thought was that we would offer anonymity to the students, shielding them from risks in offering their reflections on their school experience. We envisioned asking for the opportunity to read excerpts of the interviews at faculty meetings or working with the Faculty and Staff Diversity Committee; we thought the interviews might bring to light data that the committee would need as it worked on diversity issues. In general, the students would tell us their stories and we would lift up their voices to be heard.

Six boys, 9th and 10th graders, gathered with us for our lunch-time interview. What started as a neat, orderly interview quickly evolved into an untidy, dynamic process of its own. Over pizza, we asked our lead-off question: "Tell us what it's like to be a student of color here." We then turned on the tape recorder and listened for 45 minutes as the students talked openly, teased, laughed, and interrupted each other. As the first meeting drew to a close, dictated by the time allotted for lunch in the school, the students wanted to know when we would meet again. We set a date for the next week; this quickly evolved into a routine—an ongoing lunch-time meeting that met biweekly.

The number of boys participating ebbed and flowed, from 5 to 12, but with a core group of 8. The boys invited other students they thought might be interested; we left it to their discretion as to whom would be included. The group at different points included Jews, Hispanics, and Asians, who, along with the original African Americans, were concerned with diversity issues and the experiences of students of color in the school.

The following vignettes are drawn from the recordings of the lunch-time groups; they illustrate the steps to empowerment that the group helped foster and the process of moving from a strictly interview study to a more collaborative effort with the students.

Is This Racism?

One of the earliest uses of the group involved comparing incidents and the group members discussing among themselves and with us what was and was not racism. Working to make sense of the world they were expected to function in daily, the students raised stories to analyze, sometimes deciding an incident was an intentional act of racism, at other times deciding it was an innocent misunderstanding. Often they would pool their information about the person involved and check if there was a track record of remarks that could seem racist. Conversely, they would also swap information that would let them conclude an incident was probably a misunderstanding of some sort.

In this defining process, the boys also raised the question of what they could expect from the school administrators in dealing with racist incidents when they happened; the question the boys seemed to be asking was "will you hear us when we tell you that a racist incident has occurred?" Because the administrative staff was overwhelmingly Anglo, the boys had to cross racial and hierarchical lines to be heard. The following excerpt gives a flavor of this struggle.

The incident under discussion was that several of the boys had been called "nigger" by Craig, a student of Hispanic/Native American/Anglo origins. The boys spoke with Craig and when he did not stop the name calling, they spoke with a grade dean about it. One of the boys recounted the story.

> When the grade dean was talking to me, he said he had talked to Craig and Craig said he hadn't meant anything derogatory by it. But I don't understand that part because even after we told Craig how we felt about it, he continued to call us niggers. So I'm not sure he didn't mean it to be derogatory. The grade

dean also said that Craig was a new kid and just wanted attention.

I talked to the grade dean about three times; I retold it for him like three times just so he could get straight what happened. The grade dean said that he didn't believe that Craig meant anything by it. If that's the case, then Craig is either lying or really stupid, because we told him how we felt about this; we made it very forcibly clear, but he continued, so I'm not sure that the grade dean is correct.

It may be something unconscious on the grade dean's part; would you want to say "Yeah, some of the kids I'm responsible for, well, they're a little racist and they tend to hate people other than themselves, but you know, they're not bad." Would you want to say that? . . . He didn't do this like consciously, but I think his main point was to try and suppress it, to try and keep everybody from like—well, just kind of like blowing it off and hoping that it wouldn't happen again.

In raising the incident in the group, the boys were setting forth the contradictions in the legitimated explanation of the incident: If Craig really did not mean to be derogatory, then he must be "stupid" since he did not change his behavior after being confronted by the boys; if he was lying and the grade dean accepted his explanation, it was in lieu of facing the fact that some of the students in his domain might be racist. In their persistence in bringing up the incident with the group, the boys seemed to be asking if their perceptions of racism were correct and seeking support in learning how to deal with them. It was also a signal of a probable departure from the version of reality portrayed to them by the adult authority structure of the school. With the support of the group as a whole, they were holding on to their own sense of reality about what is or is not racism, even when their views were not legitimated by the school administration. They were becoming the experts on their own experiences.

They also seemed to be testing us as researchers and as other adults working in the school; would we feel that we had to back the party line or was criticism of administrative decisions allowed? As adult participants in the school structure, and with prior relationships with at least some of the boys, we were known as faculty versed in and committed to diversity issues; the boys had every right to expect a sympathetic hearing from us. Our willingness to be angry along with them or to hear them when they did not feel heard in other parts of the school was a further step toward validating and encouraging their voices.

Linked with a growing understanding of racism was an increased awareness of themselves as minorities; a sense of being singled out for their race brought them together as well as heightened their own growing sense of their racial identities.

Boy 1: There's like one major good thing that's come out of this (the incident with Craig), and that's like the minorities within—I know in the freshman and sophomore class—there's more unity. They seem to care what happens like to the other ones. Whereas before, like when I was down in the middle school, if something like this would happen, I can't honestly say that my brothers would have come down and like helped me out.

Boy 2: That's true, that's true.

Boy 1: But I think that this has provided more unity, not just within the Afro-American—

Boy 3: But with everyone.

Boy 1: But with everyone. I mean the Asian brothers and the Hispanic brothers.

Boy 4: I don't think there's that much racial tension in the middle school. I mean I remember all through 6th to 8th grades I saw everyone as just like—just one human race. Humans, that's all I saw. In high school I still viewed everyone as human, but it just happened that the people who were nice to me were other minorities and the people who I'm still friends with—well, some white people but they just happened to be just a little less nice to me.

Interviewer: What I'm trying to understand is if there is something about the high school climate that precipitates this kind of awareness, whether it is negative or positive; what we need to understand is what is it about this environment that brings about this sort of consciousness, this awareness that I'm different, and I'm different because, and why?

Boy 5: I really don't know what it is, it just snaps. I don't know what happened over the summer between 8th and 9th grade; I started snapping, you know, looked in the mirror and said "Hey, I'm Asian!"

Boy 1: I'm Asian and I'm proud!

Boy 5: Exactly!

Boy 2: Asian power!

Boy 3: Well, it seems like, it seems like to me the more black you get, the more flack you get. (Loud laughter from the group)

Responding to Their World

The name-calling incident was a catalyst for ongoing group discussion. By continuing to raise the incident for discussion, the boys signaled that, although the administrator involved might consider the case closed, from their point of view it still needed to be acknowledged. The repercussions of the initial exchange with the grade dean on this matter were made explicit in a conversation in the group about a month later.

> I mean right now, I mean, like there are only a few people, probably the people in this room that I would feel comfortable coming to with like the issue of diversity . . . if my diversity is being threatened, then I wouldn't—I wouldn't feel comfortable going to just any faculty member. I wouldn't feel comfortable going to that dean just because of like the way that he handled the last thing—just kind of like "forget it." I mean, I wouldn't feel comfortable going to him. . . .

Working with the idea that at least some of the administrators were not willing to deal with racist incidents, the boys used the group to discuss possible responses to the original incident with Craig and to brainstorm should something like the name-calling incident occur again. They spent a lot of time speculating that if Craig repeated his offense, there would be violence and they could not take further insults sitting down. When they first raised the idea of beating up Craig, I remember having a sick feeling in my stomach, thinking that what had started as a fairly innocent research group could be accused of fanning trouble in the school. At the same time, I felt like we had to stay with the process and let the boys hash it through and make their own decisions. What we as adults involved in the group tried to do was push the perimeters of their decision making so that they would consider any possible repercussions to their actions while it was all still hypothetical.

Initially the boys felt that because their actions would be justified, for example, Craig "deserved" to be beaten up, the consequences for them would be minimal. They believed that the school would perhaps "slap their wrists"; at most they speculated, they would be put on probation. Working to link our research questions to a larger, sociohistorical context, we were gathering information but also providing the boys with a framework for decision making. At this point, with us pushing, the boys began to connect their potential actions to the larger sociocultural frame.

Interviewer: So I hear you saying that your hands would probably be slapped but there wouldn't be any more consequences to you if you did that.

Boy 2: I think there's something a little more important than our personal consequences, like whether each one of us is put on probation. If that (beating up Craig) happened, it would damage—

Boy 1: (Interrupting.) It's going to look like a black gang took this kid out . . .

Boy 2: Yeah.

Boy 1: . . . and kicked his butt.

Interviewer: So you lose either way?

Boy 1: Yeah, it sets a precedent.

Interviewer: Yeah, that's just what I'm asking. So what are the consequences of that—let's say if it was a black gang beat up this kid. Do you think that there would be reaction aside from the faculty; I mean, do you see where the community would react?

Boy 3: Yeah, some people that were borderline before would, I assume, say "Well, I don't mind Negroes so much" but if all of a sudden a gang of Negroes went out and beat Craig up, they'd probably be pushing, saying "Look, they're trying to take over the campus" you know?

Interviewer: See, I want you guys to really think about the consequences if you really beat him up because here is an "insignifi-

cant incident" and yet, the first reflex response of you guys,
you beat up a kid like that. There's going to be a whole, almost
archetypal reflex response about this incident. You guys said
you would be just slapped a little bit, or given probation. Do
you think that you could be expelled?

Boy 4: Well, I don't even think that the most rational thing to do is
to just beat him. I don't think that it is.

There was also a growing awareness on the part of the boys that
the norms of the school culture were distinct from those represented
in other parts of the larger community. Much of their work focused
on this awareness, coupled with the sense that, while they tried to
defend the school culture to those outside of it, their presence within
the school was not without contradictions. While struggling to function in a school environment that felt in many ways like a foreign
culture, their very existence in the school and their attempt to abide
by its norms meant that they were moving away from support and
solidarity offered by groups outside of the school. In this example,
they were also moving away from one portrayal of what it means to
be "really black." Caught between at least two worlds and conflicting
senses of what it means to be a person of color, the boys struggled
to decide in what direction to move.

Boy 1: These guys that are members of the NAACP, they like talk
to me. They're all "Why haven't you beat him down yet?" And
I have to try and explain like the whole concept of like the
administration, like the consequences and everything, and they,
they say something to me like "Oh, if you were really black—
you just let him get away with that." That really upsets me.

Interviewer: So you get it at both ends.

Boy 2: There's like people within our own school, like within my
class even that—they say "Why do you guys have to act so
black; why do you have to like, always stand around together,
like in the stairwells, and always just talk to each other?"

Boy 3: Why do they have to act so white? (Laughter.)

Boy 4: Well, if we're all hanging out together that means that they're
hanging out together, doesn't it?

Interviewer: Well, what about the climate that allows for this; what in the school climate has caused you guys to just hang out together?

Rejecting the various alternatives they have thought of or have had offered to them, the boys entered a reflective period, working to center themselves and think through what felt right to them in their unique circumstances. They struggled with the tenets of "freedom of expression," wondering if they had the right to act at all, even in the face of racism. The group moved to a discussion of everyone having the right to believe whatever they wanted versus being free to act on that belief; that is, people could be prejudiced, but discrimination, the action connected to it, was an infringement on their rights. The boys were questioning the acts of the perpetrators in this incident as well as what they themselves would allow themselves in terms of a response. The following excerpt summarizes the group's conclusions on this point.

I don't agree with what he believes but I think everyone has the freedom to believe whatever they want to believe, even if it's wrong. But there's a fine line between what you believe and offending other people. I mean sensitivity is the bottom line here. If you believe it and you express it frequently and it offends other people, that's just unacceptable. He has the freedom to believe whatever he wants but he can't just go around offending people. I mean you have to be sensitive to other people's feelings.

This is the standard the boys worked to implement toward their own planning and actions, that is, how to believe what it is they believe as it relates to diversity issues, while being sensitive members of the community. They saw themselves as part of the school; with that membership came certain rights and obligations. This led them directly to the plan they finally decided on: Working to change others' beliefs. They concluded that racist actions are based on "ignorance" and that one of their goals was to see how that kind of ignorance could be replaced with knowledge.

Boy 4: I figure it's our school; it's our time to learn. It's our time to educate ourselves; it's our turn to educate each other. . . . I feel that this school is just wrong in general because they say this school is supposed to prepare us for the outside world and they don't, they don't teach about other people's history. I mean if you're going to grow up and work in this country, you're going to have to know about other people's ethnicity because you're going to work with them when you're older. I don't think they sufficiently prepare us. See everything is like ignorance. What Craig said is out of ignorance. Everyone is just ignorant about each others' backgrounds and they don't understand like—

Boy 3: (Interrupting.) —they were saying like Malcolm X was un-American.

Boy 4: Well I'm sure they weren't even reading anything about him. I mean, he grew up in a time—he was living in a time that was full of racial strife; there was a lot of tension. See, that's what people need awareness about other people's ethnicity and why they're the way they are and I mean the school, it teaches about certain types of history but not the history that directly affects us.

Boy 2: Are we going to ever have any opportunity to have like Black history courses and like Asian history courses?

Boy 3: If they do have them, it won't be while we're here.

Boy 2: I mean, like I get offended when people come up to me and say "What does that X on your hat mean? Ten? X-rated?" or something like that. I mean, I get offended kind of.

The boys had moved to a critique of the school culture as represented in the curriculum; they were linking the racist name calling with an environment that left a void where informing, enlightening knowledge should provide a safeguard from "ignorant" attacks. The lack of awareness of a school community that did not seem to connect the Xs on their tee shirts and hats to Malcolm X was read by the boys as a symbol of the ignorance they referred to as the root of the racist name calling and other incidents in the school. Not seeing themselves represented in the curriculum, they conceived the plan of beginning to ask for a more inclusive course of studies that represented a diversity of histories.

They also looked for ways to take the lead in the process of educating themselves and others; that search led them to the founding of the Minority Awareness Committee (MAC) on campus. The school had, in the past, attempted to foster a Student Diversity Committee, an organization that would work with the equivalent committee of adults in the school on diversity issues; the conclusion of the boys was that "the diversity committee just doesn't get anything done" and that was why a new, more proactive group needed to be formed, initiated by students rather than administrators and other adults in the school. After wrangling to get a vision of what the new student group should be, they drew up a proposal to have the MAC formally incorporated as a recognized organization in the school.

Boy 1: One thing that epitomized the whole reason I wanted to start the MAC was—I was passing this (petition to support the recognition of the MAC) around in history class and someone grabbed this and they were all reading it, trying to decide if they were going to sign, right? And you know Sandy Hanes, she's all "We're already aware of this stuff; we know you're minorities —what else do you want?" That totally epitomizes why I want this.

Boy 3: I think we should just like focus on educating people who are ignorant. . . . This doesn't necessarily like stereotype white people and this doesn't exclude minorities—but just target people who are ignorant—

Boy 2: (Interrupting.) Yeah, of minorities, their own culture or other cultures.

Boy 4: I think we should just unite; that's the point.

Boy 1: By becoming an officially recognized organization, we can apply to have a forum (a student-led assembly for the whole school). We can apply for a forum to educate—tell people what we are and what our point is. Because there's a lot of people, like Evan Schneider (an Anglo student) started this whole rumor about how the whole purpose of the MAC was to get rid of all the white males at school and there were like people who were just jumping on the bandwagon of that; he threatened to start a proposal that this group was going to be controversial and should not be allowed.

Boy 3: He thinks we're militants.

Boy 5: People are feeling that this is just going to be like a minority only thing; I think that's the biggest problem.

Boy 6: I don't see what the problem with minority only is.

Boy 2: One thing we need to emphasize from Mr. F.'s (the activities director) view is we need to allow Caucasians into it.

Boy 4: No!

Boy 5: But we do!

Boy 4: I don't see what the problem with minority only is.

Boy 6: Well, I think what we should do is include anyone who wants to learn about other peoples' cultures.

Interviewer: Why are the white students saying that if you have a group of minority students together it's divisive—whatever term they will use; it will create trouble and so on and so forth —which is a very historical response to any kind of organizing effort on the part of minorities. It's very important what's behind that, okay? Don't just respond to their response—then you just have emotions going on; try to understand what their feelings are, what their fears are, what their motives are. What does it relate to historically?

The birth of the MAC brought a new era to the research process. As a friendship group, the boys got together often at lunch time and continued discussions of the themes raised in the group; the tape recording of the lunch-time group represented just one slice of the multiple, ongoing discussions taking place among the boys. The lunch-time discussions became strategy sessions as the boys planned the development of the MAC; they came with typed agendas and a sense of the work they needed to accomplish to become a functioning, recognized group on campus.

Based on the work of Gutièrrez (1990), empowerment in the context of this research refers to the concept of individuals contextualizing their experiences, critically reflecting on and reformulating their worldview, and gaining a sense of personal power to join with others in changing the social order. The students in this study, hearing on an ongoing basis that they were the experts of their own experience, that their voices needed to be heard in larger arenas of the school, used the group created for data gathering as an arena for contextualizing and critiquing their experiences. They became agents for change on their own behalf and for the institution at large. The research process served, in part, as a catalyst for the students' empowerment and ownership of the change process.

Political and Methodological Implications of Empowerment

The notion of empowerment includes a sense of ownership of the process. As the energy and vision of the student group grew beyond the bounds of the lunch-time meetings, there was not even the guise that we the researchers were "in charge" of the change process. Rather, the effort became one where the researchers and the students were joined in the process of institutional change. They became collaborators producing critical knowledge aimed at concrete applications within the school. As the boys increasingly found their own way, as the MAC gained momentum and credibility within the institution, the struggle for us as researchers was one of methodologically capturing the change effort—a dynamic, fluid process that was taking place in a number of settings within the school with a variety of actors. As adults seasoned in the change process, it also meant anticipating the backlash that was a usual part of that process. Lastly, we had to work to not squelch the rush of energy released in the enthusiasm of the students' first efforts at organized institutional change—a bit worrisome to two adults feeling "responsible" for the actions, protection, and safety of a young and politically naive group of change agents.

The worry spoke to a sense of collaboration with the students, yet the unavoidable awareness of a hierarchy of adult/adolescent, faculty/student relationships. We were also aware of a movement beyond our control in the sense that we, as the researchers, did not get to call the shots; although that sense of empowered students felt "right," there were no roadmaps that we were aware of to learn how to cooperate in that empowerment across adult/student lines. The patronizing plan of us "telling their stories" was far behind us, yet there seemed to be no clear guidelines for the territory we had moved into once those subject/object lines had been blurred. How much was the initial research effort a catalyst for this sense of movement among the boys? What was our responsibility to them and to the work for change? How could we help them be wise in their efforts? What was our role, if any, with the MAC?

We were also struggling to conceptualize our own work in the change effort. The boys had formed a student organization that was publicly raising issues of diversity; if we were to collaborate in the change effort, we needed to conceptualize more clearly the adult part of that and lend our efforts to the overall work for diversity. Our original idea, that of raising the students' voices so their experiences could help inform the diversity process, was well on its way; the students had become their own spokespeople. We struggled to bring into focus our next part of the work.

The Negotiation of Multiple Roles and Multiple Levels of Reality

As a practitioner doing research in my own work site, obviously the role of the researcher was not the only one I assumed within the school. In fact, as far as the school was concerned, the stories project was an addition to my regular responsibilities, something that was "allowed" as long as I could keep up with it and my other responsibilities. What was becoming a vital part of my awareness was something that only my research colleague and I had access to: an ongoing dialogue with the boys. I felt a growing dissonance in trying to match the boys' reality, as they portrayed it, with other dialogues going on in the school. Diversity issues were addressed without taking into account the student perspective.

In the research group, we worked hard to assure the students that they were the experts on their own experiences and that we needed to hear their views to be able to work effectively for change; however, this did not necessarily translate to the way the institution as a whole went about decision making. Adults, myself among them, invested with the charge to help create policy recommendations, were not necessarily tapping into the student reality when trying to frame decisions. Yet the richness of the students' stories kept playing in my mind as I went about the rest of my work; I began to feel like I was functioning in two worlds, because there seemed to be such a gap between the students' voices and the discourse in the adult domain of the school. I was feeling more connected and safer in the student group than I was feeling in the school as a whole; this was disquieting for an adult to feel, yet somehow, on a subjective level, I knew I was encountering "real" dialogue in the student group that was not necessarily a part of my adult discussions.

I felt caught between the reality of the boys' story telling and the sanctioned discourse of the school. Although as an institution we were endorsing the movement toward multiculturalism, I was not sure that what the school had in mind encompassed my read of what that movement toward diversity would mean. I was seeing diversity as a challenge to a hierarchical structure in the school, where we would grow to a place of shared decision making based on the voices of the real "experts," those whose lives were impacted by our policies. Because I was hearing very little in the public discourse of the school that seemed to be equating the diversity movement with power sharing, I was all too aware that I risked being marginalized from the rest of the school community if I expressed my own conclusions. But I was also aware that there was no going back, that the boys' stories framed what I was hearing in the public discourse and helped create a sense of dissonance for me. My choice seemed to be either to discount the boys' stories or to confront some of the taboo areas in the school; neither alternative looked appealing.

Just as the students had times when they were meeting without either of the researchers being involved, both my research colleague and I were involved in other activities in the school that directly touched on issues of diversity. When did our researcher hats come off and our roles as practitioners emerge? Was it possible to separate the two?

I remember sitting in a meeting with some of the parents of children of color who were proposing some policy changes for the school handbook that identified and responded to racist attitudes and incidents in the school; the dialogue involved representatives from the school administration and the Faculty/Staff Diversity Committee. As an intense dialogue flowed back and forth, I found myself jotting down the equivalent of field notes, trying to capture the sense of the conversation on paper. I instinctively did this, thinking it would inform some of my thinking about how an institution creates an environment where all can thrive.

Ultimately I stopped trying to take notes during the meetings because I found it distracting to my role of participant; it was hard for me to engage in the dialogue fully while trying to record it on paper. Although not a part of my formal research, the dialogue that the field notes recorded was part of the larger contextualization of the boys' stories, outlining in broader strokes the school's work regarding diversity issues. I struggled with whether these field notes were "usable" data, because I did not feel that I had "permission" for such note taking; I was very aware that the others in the group saw me as a participant, as a member of the Faculty/Staff Diversity Committee, rather than a researcher. It felt like one thing to record a student group and another thing to cast the lens of inquiry onto a group process that potentially portrayed representatives of the school administration in a less than favorable light.

A number of the boys' parents were directly involved in these parents' groups; in the boys' group, we began to recognize a flow of information to the students as parents processed the meetings at home. Because the school and the parent community were struggling to be allies over issues of diversity rather than ending up as divided and warring factions, it was particularly tricky in the group to decide, as adults, just how open to be. Our own emotions and spirits ebbed and flowed, dependent on our perceptions of how much "progress" we were making and how much was possible; how much of our concern should be shared with students? These questions caused us to wonder how to collaborate with students, how to work across hierarchical lines of adults/adolescents, teachers/students, and how to be representatives of the school while critiquing it.

Both my research colleague and I had been appointed to the Faculty/Staff Diversity Committee, charged to bring some leadership to the school on multicultural issues. It was within this smaller arena that I began to take some risks, to deepen the dialogue regarding movement toward a truly multicultural organization. With a knot in my stomach, I tried, at meetings, to be as "real" as I could, while simultaneously assessing the level of risk to me. Aware that the boys' stories were taking place in an environment that I interacted with on a daily basis, I wondered how to use their stories to inform the committee process. I also wondered how, through the decisions we recommended to the school administration, the diversity committee might work toward making the environment one where all students, as well as those in our boys' group, would thrive. The dilemma methodologically was how to use the data that we were collecting to inform the decision making that was simultaneously occurring in other arenas in the school.

We had been recording all the lunch-time groups, and I had hired someone to transcribe them, but there was no time to pour over the transcripts systematically and to make sense of all the themes, much less to use computer software like "Ethnograph" to code them. If I wanted to be in the larger dialogue already occurring in the school, I had to take what opportunities presented themselves, whether I was "ready" or not. Our first round of data analysis consisted mostly of the quick debriefing my colleague and I went through immediately following the lunch groups—the same time frame that ended group and took the students back to class imposed itself on us as well. This sense of snatching time for research in the midst of an already busy schedule was an ever-present struggle. We compared a sense of what we had heard, what meanings we could make out of it, and what plans we would make next. Although I wished for a leisurely hour for this debriefing and meaning making, in reality we had about 20 minutes.

It felt overwhelming to be working to make sense of all that I was hearing from the students, "the data," while simultaneously needing that burgeoning understanding to inform courses of possible action being proposed in other avenues in the school. I had a longing for some order, a sense of wanting to finish one area (i.e., data gathering and analysis) before I needed to use it. I had not anticipated that moving into an action research framework would feel so uncomfortable, that I would need to speak in the forums offered to me while feeling that I myself only had partial knowledge. I longed for the mythology of a cleaner research project, where I would speak from a safe, distant place about my data and the change effort would carefully flow in a systematic way, informed by the power of the research results. I had not expected the reality to be so much messier than the research I had done in other sites where, as an outsider, I entered a research site and studied it but was not intimately involved in it.

For me, as a school employee, this kind of intimate involvement with my research site raised issues of vulnerability as I struggled with how to be honest to my own perceptions, increasingly informed by the student stories, while not sounding so dissenting at school meetings that I would be discounted or face negative sanctions. I felt accountable to the students, in the face of their terrible honesty, to be true to the reality they were portraying, although also aware that it was not easy to be "real" in many settings in the institution. I was being changed in the process of listening to the students, aware that I had an opportunity that others in the school did not have at that time, but I also felt that my growing awareness was creating a gap between myself and other adults in the school.

Doing this type of research with another colleague was critical. Our relationship provided one space in the school where my worlds could come together, where I could be real with another adult without risk. It was a safe space where I could process and integrate the data, allow it to impact me, and feel the support of another adult in the same school community. Sometimes I felt exhilarated by doing this research; at other times it felt like an "add on," something else to tackle in the midst of too many other demands. At times I found myself wondering why I had ever gotten myself into it.

Transformation Becomes a Kind of War

Schon's (1971, cited in Holly, 1989) concept of dynamic conservatism leads to the expectation that, as a group within an institution works for change, there will be an equal force working to maintain the status quo. "Because it sees every effort at transformation as an attack, transformation becomes a kind of war" (Schon, 1971, cited in Holly, 1989, p. 80).

In mid-December, my research colleague received a death threat via the computerized communication system of the school. Explicitly racist in its contents, the threat was signed "Sincerely, KKK." By January, the MAC had received a similar threat, signed by the "Aryan Control Committee." The school struggled not to make the incidents public in the hopes of increasing the chance of apprehending the perpetrators. Eventually local and federal investigators were called to investigate. Phones were tapped when members of the boys' group and my research colleague started receiving threatening phone calls at home. Headlines spilled across the local newspaper, giving daily updates of the events; television crews came to campus, shoving microphones in the faces of the boys from the group.

The headmaster addressed the school community in an all-school assembly, reassuring students and faculty alike that all that could be done was being done; he reiterated that the school stood behind its efforts to continue working on diversity issues. A middle school student, a Hispanic girl, discovered a threatening note in her locker; the contents were similar to notes delivered to the MAC. We organized a vigil, a candlelight show of support for those threatened, along with an open microphone for students, faculty, and staff to voice their fears, disappointments, and outrage. Parent meetings were held to discuss the incidents, the increased security, and the climate that might allow such a thing to happen.

The ranks of the MAC swelled, and it held its own public forums to let students speak not only of the current, blatant incidents but also of what life was like on a day-to-day basis for students of color in the school. Parents of the boys in the group called me, worried and sleepless, living with tapped telephones and hoping to stave off further threats to their children. Emotionally torn and exhausted, my research colleague took a short leave of absence from the school. The investigators found nothing conclusive; we tried to resume school in a somewhat normal fashion. That spring, two bomb threats led to the evacuation of the campus, and we made the newspapers once again. Were these threats related to the earlier, threatening notes? No one knew. Did the bomb threats contribute to a feeling of danger? Definitely. We grimly worked to get to the end of the school year.

Epilogue

The following school year was quiet. The MAC was reconfigured and changed its name to the Humanity Interaction Team (HIT). A few of the original members are still a part of it; others are lobbying for a Black Student Union on campus to continue defining what it means to be an African American in a predominately Anglo environment.

My research colleague, originally on leave from the public schools, left at the end of our eventful school year. As part of a parents' group, he continues a dialogue on race issues with the headmaster. His presence and model of how to be authentic and vulnerable are missed on campus.

The student coordinators of the HIT have asked me to work with them on a weekend retreat, helping them talk across racial lines. The work continues. I continue to interview and try to understand the movement of diversifying in a school context.

I spent a lot of time thinking through how much the organizing of a group of students of color contributed to a tumultuous school year and how much was just the reality of living in a racist society. I wondered how much I put students at risk just by asking the question, "Tell me what it's like being a student of color here." There is no real way to ever know. What we do know is that, as we work to raise voices, others work to silence them. As we make the invisible visible, others resist seeing. As we learn to work together, collaboratively, we are a threat; that threat does not go unnoticed. When the racist threats occurred, the fledgling MAC was in a position to respond; as an already organized entity, it linked with others in the school and worked to use the threats as an educational tool. This is not the kind of research that measures cause and effect, but it is the kind of research that points to possibilities.

Discussion

The scenario outlined here by Herr is an extreme example of the "spillover" effect referred to earlier in this chapter; practitioner research takes place in a large, institutional context and is not necessarily containable to one corner of the practitioner's world. Following the vagaries of action research, the researcher, at best, can prepare to follow where the sense of empowerment is leading—often out of the corners and into the larger institution.

Although the original research was conceptualized to improve practice, that is, to help create a more nurturing environment for diverse students, its actual evolution, including the sense of empowerment of the students, expanded the research agenda to one where research and action became a single process. Rather than the change effort following a linear equation where the data are gathered and then are applied to problem-solving, the research question acted as a catalyst, generating a theme—racism—for further exploration and education. The results of this kind of exploration were immediately applied to the students' situation: They felt that racist name calling reflected an ignorance of diverse histories, an ignorance supported by the narrow range of the school's current curriculum; they decided to work to educate the ignorant. The course of action came from a critical look at the world in which they functioned and a linking of their situation to a larger, sociohistorical context (i.e., the historical interaction between the dominant culture and people of color and an examination of their "reflex responses" to racist incidents in the light of this sociohistorical view). The courses of action eventually chosen resulted from this analysis, coupled with a sense of the students' own empowerment—"it's our school; it's our time to learn."

The challenge for researchers is to become just another participant, rather than the ones "in charge" of the change effort. By encouraging a sense of empowering participation, researchers relinquish a sense of control of the research/action and are committed instead to shared decision making, with their voice being just one in the chorus calling for change.

But Is It Research?

Some might say this has been a compelling narrative of the possibilities and risks of empowerment, but how does it speak to a larger community, whether of practitioners or academics or others? What are the "findings"? Where is the theory? Is this research? Imagine the comments a reviewer of an academic educational journal might make!

Most practitioners who work in schools like the one described will find these questions humorous. They will see them as a spoof on how academics, even qualitative ones, think about research. Practitioners bring to narratives a wealth of tacit knowledge and a set of similar preoccupations that resonate with many of the situations and insights described. Only another practitioner can know how it feels to be in the situation described. This narrative will be received by practitioners with an empathy and poignancy lacking in the hard-nosed questions about findings, theory, and method. As practitioners read narratives like this, they are actively engaged in the process of naturalistic generalization described in Chapter 2.

Drawing on our categories from Chapter 2, the internal validity of the study is established in the account. The democratic validity of the study, or the inclusion of multiple voices or perspectives, was achieved through the inclusion of the perspective of the students of color. Although not included in the above account, data from school committees and the administration were also gathered.

Outcome validity was established through the continual rethinking of the dilemmas presented, which ultimately resulted in a permanent student diversity organization. Questions of diversity were not "solved," but a mechanism for dealing with diversity issues from the students' perspective was a concrete result of the study.

Process validity was established as Herr discussed her ongoing decision making about methods. In practitioner research, process validity refers to finding methodological adaptations that fit the contingencies of the setting and the flow of action. Ongoing learning was established through the continuation of the HIT, which indicates that the learning will continue. This type of validity has not been achieved at the institutional level, although real organizational learning is probably beyond the purview of a single action research project.

Catalytic validity resulted in an increased level of consciousness both in the students of color and in other students in the school, as well as, although to a lesser extent, in some teachers and administrators.

Finally, dialogic validity was achieved through the collaboration between colleagues. The two colleagues were able to check each others' perceptions; because the collaboration was interracial, some degree of perception check was provided for the white, Anglo researcher.

However, in spite of the external validity of the naturalistic generalizations and the internal validity gauged from the above criteria, it is still fair to ask if there is any generation or testing of theory in Herr's study. Although perhaps not generating new theory, the study does confirm and extend work that identifies the problems of change residing in disjunctions between discursive and "deep" levels of organizational functioning (Argyris et al., 1985; Robinson, 1993).

This study shows that the politics of practitioner research, and of change generally, are internal and external, complex and multilayered. The relationship between these levels is significant; once one has tapped into the "deep" or "real" level of an organization, the discursive level becomes more and more transparent. Of course, one could argue that neither level is "real" in that both are social constructions; however, they are constructed socially for different purposes. As Anderson (1990) suggests, the discursive level is constructed in such a way as to support the status quo and legitimate the organization to its environment. The deep level, in this case the students' worldview, is constructed out of the students' experiences in a racist society. These different constructions also exist within a context of hierarchical and unequal distributions of power.

This organizational duality often leads to alienation (or worse) for both students and practitioners who attempt to point out the disjunctions between levels. Students may end up communicating their sense of dissonance by "acting out" behavior, leading to sanctions and possible expulsion from the institution. Proactive practitioners are often silenced through labeling (e.g., "negative," "trouble-maker," "feminist," "angry," "abrasive") and other forms of marginalization. In this way the deep level of organizational life is kept invisible to the rest of the institution, thwarting any meaningful change. As practitioners, we need to keep asking ourselves what is worth the risks involved and how committed we are to our institutions; deeply valuing ourselves and our educational settings means a willingness to keep risking raising our voices and working to help them be heard.

5

Qualitative Research Approaches
for Everyday Realities

Teacher researchers can revolutionize professional practice by viewing themselves as potentially the most sophisticated research instruments available. The cult of the expert will undoubtedly be uncomfortable with such research populism.

(Kincheloe, 1991, p. 30)

In this chapter we discuss a wide variety of techniques that qualitative researchers use. Other authors have described, in detail, each type of qualitative technique, but we present a more general approach and give ample references to enable the reader to pursue a particular procedure in more depth. We also incorporate examples of how these various approaches have been adapted and used by practitioner researchers.

Qualitative research has become well known in educational circles in recent years, as much for its naturalistic approach to research questions and techniques as for the implications of its alternative paradigm structure. Qualitative and quantitative research are often compared; both develop a research question or focus, define a population to work with, collect and analyze data, and present conclusions. Both involve theory, albeit at differing points in the research. However, they go about the process very differently and have developed into different paradigms of "how to do the work." A third paradigm of research, practitioner research, is in the process of being developed; this research uses elements of the qualitative and quantitative research paradigms, as well as ways to conduct research in concrete settings and theoretical contexts.

Research techniques and approaches must always be tempered by practice and seen through a filter of one's own environment and needs. How you can improve your practice, what you can contribute to the field of knowledge about learning, curriculum, teaching, and running a school necessitates an adaptable research methodology. It is important for practitioner researchers to remember that, despite traditional qualitative techniques, "The 'sedentary wisdom' of long-established traditions offers legitimation rather than liberation; the biggest breakthroughs in scientific thinking have often required a break with investigative traditions rather than blind allegiance to them" (Wolcott, 1992, p. 17).

Practitioner research is a significant way of knowing about schools. Cochran-Smith and Lytle (1993) feel that "inquiry by individual teachers and communities of teacher researchers realigns their relationships to knowledge and to the brokers of knowledge and also necessitates a redefinition of the notion of a knowledge base for teaching" (p. 43). This applies to all types of practitioner researchers, not just teachers.

As we describe the various techniques and strategies in qualitative research, remember that, as a practitioner researcher, you will adapt, refine, and build upon these "traditional" approaches. Cochran-Smith and Lytle (1993) articulate this view:

> We argue that we need to develop a different theory of knowledge for teaching, a different epistemology that regards inquiry by teachers themselves as a distinctive and important way of knowing about teaching. From this perspective, fundamental questions about knowing, knowers, and what can be known would have different answers. Teachers would be among those who have the authority to know—that is, to construct Knowledge (with a capital K) about teaching, learning, and schooling. And what is worth knowing about

teaching includes teachers "ways of knowing" or what teachers, who are researchers in their own classrooms, can know through systematic subjectivity. (p. 43)

Systematic subjectivity is a necessary component of all research, including practitioner research; the systematic nature of inquiry must be emphasized to be useful to the teacher, the principal, the counselor, the students, other stakeholders such as parents, and the larger educational community.

Traditionally, the three core techniques in qualitative research have been broadly labeled: interviews, observations, and archives and documents. Practitioner researchers are already adapting these techniques, as well as developing new ones. A newer technique is the use of personal narratives or stories as data. Another is the use of journals and diaries, begun in high school English and writing classes and now becoming an important part of many practitioner studies. These examples come from the humanities rather than the social sciences, where most of the rest of qualitative research originates. Many practitioner researchers are pushing the edges of what has heretofore been accepted as "appropriate" data and creating new areas that enhance the research process and the data gathered.

Assumptive Modes

The three initial categories of qualitative data, as well as the newer ones, share four general assumptive modes that range on a continuum. Qualitative research is at one end of the continuum and quantitative research is on the opposite end, but there is much room for overlap (see Figure 5.1). LeCompte and Preissle (1993) elaborate these assumptive modes.

Assumptive Mode 1: Induction to Deduction

Induction to deduction refers to the place of theory in a research study. A qualitative, inductive study begins by collecting data; after the initial period, it seeks theoretical propositions that match and help elucidate the data. For example, a researcher observes in a classroom, sees the behaviors of the children in the room and on the

QUALITATIVE   QUANTITATIVE

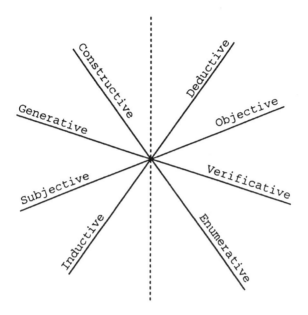

Figure 5.1. The Assumptive Modes
SOURCE: Adapted by Mia Cramer from LeCompte and Preissle, 1993.

playground, and begins to notice gender differences in the way they play. She would then go to the published research literature and seek a theory that helps explain the data she has, and then link these data to the literature and research. On the other hand, quantitative, deductive research begins with a theory, and matches it to a body of data. For example, if a theory says that girls do worse than boys in geometry, then the researcher would go into a high school and administer a test to all the ninth graders in geometry, or look at all the scores on tests previously taken by the students. The researcher seeks data to confirm the theory.

Assumptive Mode 2: Generation to Verification

Generation to verification refers to the position of evidence or data within a research study, as well as the extent to which results from the study may be generalized to other groups. For example, a qualitative researcher observes and talks to children, sees their behavior in the classroom, adds this data to other data, and then synthesizes the data and builds constructs that help explain the behaviors. Qualitative research does not seek to generalize one study to all other similar studies; instead it seeks to explain behavior in one setting, which, if it reminds the reader of his or her own setting, has been successful. For example, an elementary school practitioner researcher describes a classroom and playground of an elementary school and shows how the gender system works in that cultural scene. The reader of this study is reminded of his own classroom, and wonders if the same gender system is at play in his high school lab as was described by the elementary school teacher. The initial study has "rung" true for the reader and perhaps encouraged another study.

Verification in quantitative research seeks to authenticate or test propositions developed elsewhere and attempts to generalize beyond the scope of a single study.

Assumptive Mode 3: Construction to Enumeration

Construction to enumeration refers to how the study's units of analysis are formulated and delineated. For qualitative research, this involves discovering and developing, or constructing, analytical constructs based on the data; the researcher synthesizes all the data collected and puts it into categories that emerge from the data. In the abstraction process, the researcher moves the data into theoretical or more generalizable constructs and seeks to discover analytic categories from that particular stream of behaviors. Enumeration is the process whereby a quantitative researcher uses previously derived units of analysis and systematically counts data within these units.

Assumptive Mode 4: Subjective to Objective

The final mode is subjective to objective. Qualitative research, by its very nature, implies working in a naturalistic or real setting rather than an experimental or laboratory setting; practitioner researchers are certainly in the midst of their own natural settings. This gives the researcher a sense of immediacy and a depth of understanding by virtue of his or her position and by the chosen research paradigm. The position also demands that the researcher balance his or her "observer bias" with the "reactivity of participants." In other words, when a practitioner researcher is wearing her researcher hat, her colleagues will react to that hat as much as to her accustomed role of teacher or counselor; the teacher, as a researcher, needs to see things both as a researcher and as a staff member of the school. This can be problematic; for example, a practitioner researcher is interviewing, and the participant being interviewed gets confused as to which role he is speaking to, fellow staff member or researcher.

Practitioner researchers can work with subjectivity by presenting both initial assumptions and subjective reactions to events; in effect, presenting audiences with both preconceptions and postconceptions. Qualitative researchers address subjectivity by incorporating and openly discussing it; quantitative researchers address subjectivity by attempting to exhume it from themselves and their study by design and statistics (LeCompte & Preissle, 1993).

One final point should be made about the subjective to objective continuum. Part of subjectivity in research involves the use of the terms *emic* and *etic*. An emic study is one in which a researcher describes cultural and behavioral patterns as they are viewed by the participants in the study rather than by the researcher and the research literature. The people studied create the categories of their experiences, not the researcher. This is called, variously, emic, phenomenological, or subjective research, and is considered a critical juncture in the difference between the paradigms of qualitative and quantitative research (LeCompte & Preissle, 1993). Cochran-Smith and Lytle (1993) make a strong argument for the uniquely emic positioning of a practitioner researcher: "Teacher researchers are uniquely positioned to provide a truly emic, or insider's, perspective that makes visible the ways that students and teachers together construct knowledge and curriculum" (p. 43).

Cochran-Smith and Lytle (1993) present anthropologist Geertz's (1983) discussion of the difficulties nonpractitioner researchers have in truly representing the emic categories of their participants. Geertz feels that anthropologists cannot really represent "local knowledge" —what inhabitants see—but can only represent what they see through, that is, their interpretive perspectives on their own experiences.

Cochran-Smith and Lytle turn this around for practitioner researchers and elaborate on the fact that local knowledge is what teachers come to know through their own research and what communities of teacher researchers come to know when they build knowledge collaboratively. Teacher research, and we broaden the idea to mean practitioner research, can contribute a fundamental reconceptualization of the notion of knowledge for teaching. Teacher researchers can reinvent the conventions of interpretive social science, much as feminist and minority researchers have done by making problematic the relationships of researchers and researched, knowledge and authority, and subject and object (Cochran-Smith & Lytle, 1993).

We offer, at this point, a broad-based example of practitioner research that exemplifies many characteristics of qualitative research and that highlights the assumptive modes. This vignette is from Ann Strommen, a literacy and early childhood specialist. She worked with four groups of kindergarten and 1st grade children in a Chapter I Reading pullout program. The children who came to her room for 1 hour each day were referred by their teachers because of problems in reading. Strommen, with a colleague, developed a series of contracts that the children worked on each week perfecting skills introduced at the beginning of the week. All contracts involved reading and writing.

After fulfilling the tasks of the contract, the children were free to engage in one of the many free-time activities in the room. Strommen did not have a clear sense of which activities the children were most often engaged in. Her research question, therefore, was developed to enhance her exploration of what the children did during self-selection time. She says:

> I wanted a question that would be helpful to me as a teacher and would be within my capabilities. I had little time to observe the room and the sixteen children in it at any given time. Ann (Nihlen) visited the classroom and together we devised a spot observation technique. I then worked on a recording sheet that allowed me to scan the room at various predetermined times and record where the students were and what they were doing. I began this observation and immediately found it necessary to revise and refine the recording

sheet. I had originally thought it would be most advantageous to know in what areas of the room the children were. I felt location would tell me what they were doing. I quickly remembered that children could, for instance, write in the reading area, and solve puzzles in the art area. My revised recording sheet now listed the activities the children could be engaged in. The qualitative approach allowed me not only to modify and change my observations, based on the reality of my classroom, but to feel comfortable changing my focus as the data led me. The research class supported my efforts to be led by, rather than lead, the data. Later I added the category of sex to the recording sheet to see if any gender differences would show up. (Strommen, 1991, p. 34)

One of the many things that Strommen discovered was that one-half of the children were not finishing their contracts in time to have self-selection. This came as a surprise to her, until she realized that it also meant that the other half was finishing and making self-selection choices; this group became her database. From a pilot study Strommen had conducted earlier in the semester, she knew that all the teachers in the school thought that self-selection was important and that most provided for it daily. Working inductively, Strommen went to the library and began the review of the literature:

If research supports self-selection activities as a vehicle to help develop literacy in kindergarten and first grade students, my teammate and I would probably need to make some adjustments. One would be to change the schedule to allow time for more students to participate in self-selection activities. Another change might be to separate or rearrange their block, puzzle and game activity areas since it is so popular. (Strommen, 1991, p. 35)

Strommen learned through this process that she could do research that was directly relevant to her classroom and her teaching. She came to realize that qualitative research provides data that can be analyzed in many different ways and that provide a variety of answers, sometimes to questions the researcher did not know he or she had. Strommen decided, using both a constructive and a subjective mode, to let the data lead her. She also discovered that she could use what she learned immediately for the benefit of her students. In addition, she could share the general results with a wider audience of teachers and researchers by talking about and publishing the data. Strommen was surprised that she had learned to do research, because, as she said, "Who would have thought a little old grey-headed kindergarten teacher could do research?" (Strommen, 1991, p. 35).

This vignette is also an excellent example of the action research spiral discussed throughout this book.

The Research Question

As one embarks on research, the first step to undertake in the preparation for a study is the articulation of the research question. In qualitative research, this is an open-ended, general statement identifying the area of interest. For example, if an elementary school classroom teacher is curious about self-selection time and how children use it, the question or formulation of the research could be "What are children doing during self-selection time?" or, for a high school teacher with an integrated Special Education/regular education classroom, "Are students from both groups integrated during social times?"

After the researcher has written down the initial question, he or she must think about how to find answers to this question. In this way, the questions always drive the study, never the reverse. Many practitioner researchers value "talking through" the question with colleagues and other practitioner researchers. This can give a broader perspective on the question, methods, and data; and other reflections and individual experiences can prove invaluable. Several examples of relying on these "critical friends" are in Chapter 3; see also Christman et al., in press; Evans, 1989; Russell, 1992; and Stubbs, 1989.

In the following sections, we describe what is commonly meant when interviews, observations, and archival and document retrieval techniques are mentioned by a researcher. Each method can be done separately as a study; however, combining the techniques in differ-

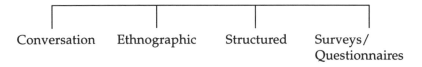

Figure 5.2. Types of Interviews

ent ways, called triangulation of data, allows the researcher to maximize time and to see the same scene from different angles. For practitioner researchers, this can provide a very important perspective. It helps the researcher separate from a classroom or school that he or she knows intimately, and it allows the researcher to "make the familiar strange" (Erickson, 1973)—strange enough to see with new eyes (instead of the usual perspective).

Methods

Interviews

Interviews have been variously described as a conversation with another person, a verbal questionnaire, or a life story. This wide-ranging definition implies the variety of techniques one could use in conducting an interview with another person or persons.

Interviews are a good tool to use when one wishes to know how a person feels about events that have happened or are happening. They are also important in gaining a perspective on how others understand and interpret their reality. Interviewing assumes a skill in listening and a nonthreatening manner in asking questions.

We discuss several types of interviewing here: the open-ended interview; the questionnaire-type or directed interview; and surveys, questionnaires, checklists, rating scales, and inventories (see Figure 5.2). In addition, we discuss two products of interview studies: the oral history and the narrative story.

Some disadvantages of interviewing are:

1. It is difficult to get a list of good, sequential questions together.

2. Response rates are often low due to fear of discovery and lack of anonymity, particularly within a school or district and for "hot" issues; neither the questioner nor the respondents may want something in writing.

3. Some people do not answer questions honestly and therefore skew the data.

Regardless of the type of interview you choose, certain tasks must be accomplished before beginning to ensure a successful product.

1. To begin, you should contact the potential participant and discuss the possibility of interviewing him or her. Tell the participant why and what you hope to accomplish, and the purpose of the research. It is best to have had face-to-face contact before the interview; that makes both of you more comfortable. Both you and the participant must see you as a researcher as well as practitioner. This is an additional role for you as a practitioner. How to help people understand that the role will change and shift is very important, and very difficult. The difficulty comes in figuring out how you can let colleagues and other stakeholders know what role you are in at any given time.

2. In recent years, researchers and the researched have developed certain courtesies to protect each party. The consent form is one of these; it may be required by your district or school. As a researcher, you must provide some kind of consent form for the interviewee to read and sign. The consent describes the research you will be conducting, how many times you might interview the person, the use of recording equipment, some guarantee of the person's anonymity if he or she desires this, reassurance that he or she can quit the research at any time, and phone numbers where he or she can reach you outside of school. Both you and the interviewee should sign two copies; then you keep one and the interviewee keeps one. The form should be signed prior to the first interview. You should be there to answer any questions the interviewee may have; this assures you that he or she has read the form and understands the serious intent of your research and the gift of permission to interview him or her. Since some

school districts require such forms, check to ascertain what needs to be done and how to do it to meet whatever guidelines apply.

One important way that practitioner researchers gather data is in the informal settings of the school, the casual conversations in the teacher's lounge or by the mailboxes, and the public discourse of meetings. Many practitioners speak of the difficulty in deciding what is permissible to use and record as research, particularly if they decide to share with colleagues or publish for public consumption. Try to build your own guidelines and let others know how you wish to proceed.

3. Prepare your questions. No matter how general or how specific you intend to be, be sure that you have more than enough questions or topic areas to fill the time. Try to make them expository questions rather than yes or no questions. Start out with a question that is easy to answer, often about the interviewee himself or herself.

   Interviews done on the run in informal settings usually are not taped; you must jot down the main points as soon as possible after the interaction. It is amazing how quickly one forgets.

4. Check your equipment before you start the interview. Cassette tape recorders are inexpensive and common, and most are battery powered. A cassette recorder with a tape counter is most useful for later analysis. If you are planning on a half-hour interview or an hour interview, use a 90-minute tape so you do not have to turn the tape over often or replace it. Carry extra tapes and batteries.

5. Make sure that the room you have chosen is as quiet as possible. If it is in the school, try to find an out-of-the-way place where few people walk through, and try to position the participant so that people cannot catch his or her eye.

6. Chat with the participant while you set up and arrange the tape recorder; this will make both of you feel more relaxed. If you are using an external microphone, be sure to explain this to the interviewee.

7. Begin the interview by starting the tape, checking to see if it is running, and speaking into the microphone, giving your name, the participant's name or pseudonym, and the date and location

of interview. Ask the interviewee to say something into the microphone, stop the tape, rewind it, and check to see that both voices are being heard. Then proceed with your first question. Take notes during the interview in the briefest form if at all; you want to be a good listener. Keep your eyes in an interviewing mode—depending on the culture, on or off the participant, or to one side.

8. As you end the interview, ask the participant if he or she would like to add something to what he or she has said. After that, turn off the tape and thank the person for the time and thought. If you plan another interview, talk briefly about when you will call to set up another interview.

9. Label the tapes before or as soon as possible after the interview. Label clearly and precisely the name, date, and project.

10. Now that you have a taped interview, transcribe and analyze it. Allow approximately 4 hours of transcribing for each hour of recorded interview. Many researchers pay professional transcribers to do this task, for it is labor intensive. A good typist and transcriber can make short work of it, and they certainly earn their money.

Another technique to handle reviewing and analyzing tapes, particularly if you have a lot of tapes and/or little money or time for transcribing them yourself, is to index the tapes. First listen to all the tapes. Then pick out themes of interest and relevance to the research question. Record on an index card the interviewee name, the date, and the number on the tape counter where the section you are interested in occurs. As you develop categories based on the data, you may have to listen again to the tapes, but this is a less expensive way to analyze the interviews.

In the latter sections of this chapter we discuss various methods for analyzing the interview. It is important to read these sections before conducting an actual interview; they will help you formulate questions to ask and to structure the analysis of your data.

The Ethnographic Interview

The open-ended interview is also called an ethnographic interview because of its original home within ethnographic research in anthropology. To grasp the design and intentions of this interview strategy, one must understand a few things about ethnography. Ethnography is considered both a process and a product. As a product, it gives a reader a comprehensive, holistic description of a cultural scene such as a tribal village, a homeless shelter, or a classroom. The core of ethnography is its concern with the meaning of actions and events to the people we seek to understand. The purpose is to provide a cultural interpretation of a scene within a culture; culture in this sense refers to the acquired knowledge that people use to interpret experience and generate social behavior (Spradley, 1979).

The ethnographic interview is a technique for gathering data for an ethnography, but it also can be, and frequently is, used in other types of qualitative research. In the process of interviewing, this technique develops descriptive open-ended questions, or what Spradley (1980) calls "descriptive" and "grand tour" questions. These types of questions enable the participants to talk about what they do and to build their own emic categories for their stories. An example of this can be found in the Emerson Elementary School Oral History Project. This project came out of the work of teachers developing a professional development school who wanted, after the first 5 years, to reflect on their practice over the years (see Holmes Group, 1990). The teachers and Nihlen collaboratively conducted a series of interviews, the former as practitioner researchers, the latter as a university professor. An interviewer asked a staff member "Tell me about your experiences at Emerson School." The answering of such a question can lead to what Spradley calls *mini-tour* questions (e.g., "You indicated that Emerson was a professional development school, can you describe its history for me?"), as well as *example* questions (e.g., "Can you give me an example of site-based management?"), *experience* questions (e.g., "Could you tell me about some of your experiences on the School Leadership Team?"), and *native-language* questions (e.g., "What would teachers call this self-governing group?"). In this case, because the interviewer and interviewee were often both teachers and both knew things about the school, the interviewee was allowed and encouraged to tell her or his own story about the school.

Spradley (1980) describes two other kinds of questions: *structural* and *contrast* questions. After each interview, the researcher must

analyze the data already collected before conducting further interviews. This ongoing process of collecting data, analyzing and reflecting
on data, and then going forward with additional collection of data is
called "grounded theory" by Glaser and Strauss (1967). We also call
it good common sense. When collecting qualitative data, one should
pause frequently to reflect and analyze. This provides an opportunity
to use the action research model or spiral of plan, act, observe, reflect, revise. See Chapter 2 for a more detailed description of the action
research model and Chapter 3 for an example. Also see Kemmis and
McTaggart (1982).

Structural questions, asked in the second interview with a participant, enable the interviewer to discover information about how
participants organize the knowledge they described in the first
interview. For example, the interviewee might be talking about her
classroom and mention that she has six reading groups; the interviewer could ask "What characterizes the different groups you
mentioned?" or "What other kinds of groups do you have?"

Contrast questions are asked in later interviews to understand
what participants mean by the terms they use. If the above teacher
is talking about her reading groups and mentions that she also has
groups for other activities, the interviewer could ask a contrast question to help understand all the things the interviewee means when
she talks about groups (e.g., "What is the difference in the groups
for art and the groups for reading?"). Or a principal might discuss
his professional development school and how staff participate in
governance, and the interviewer would ask "What's the difference
between governance at your school and other schools?"

Spradley (1980) carefully leads a new interviewer through the
steps of asking questions and then analyzing the data produced; his
book is an excellent resource for the beginner. In The Final Analysis
section of this chapter, we discuss Spradley's ideas, and we suggest
that you read this section before undertaking any interviewing. Knowing how you might construct categories out of your data to analyze
it is important information to keep in mind when interviewing. It
can save many unnecessary hours of extra analysis.

The ethnographic interview is a core technique and can be used
alone or in combination with other techniques such as observation
to build multiple-methods studies, discussed later in this chapter.

Oral History and Narrative Stories

Oral histories document the history of events and processes in the words of the people who participated. Carlos Vasquez discusses their use:

> Historians utilize them to get at the "truth behind the facts" of archival research, anthropologists to solicit ethnographic data attainable in no other way, linguists to document the uniqueness and fluidity of changing languages and dialects, sociologists to capture the most intimate and subjective nuances of social processes. For the scholar of human communications, oral history interviews provide the means by which to study how people understand one another and why that understanding so often breaks down. (University of New Mexico, Oral history Program, 1991, p. 2)

Oral history, is experiencing renewed interest from many researchers; practitioner researchers are no exception. Participants in the Emerson Elementary School Oral History Project sought a research technique that would tell the story of the staff in their own words. Oral histories, conducted by teachers interviewing each other, allow voices to be heard clearly.

Many feminists and minorities are interested in this research tool because it helps keep the voice of the interviewee intact and helps reveal a story from the teller's own perspective. In more traditional interviewing, controlled by an outsider who asks the questions, voices have been lost.

Janesick (1990) researched deaf culture in Washington, D.C., and asked deaf students how they managed both academically and in the job market. She used oral histories as part of her research plan.

Some good references on oral history are Lanman and Mehafy (1988), Dunaway and Baum (1984), and Gluck and Patai (1991). See also the literary oral histories of Hurston (1935, 1985). Terkel (1974, 1980) provides wonderful examples of this technique.

The *narrative story*, on the other hand, has become a method for studying teaching that is concerned with "the personal histories of participants embedded within the social history of schools and schooling" and is solicited and collected not merely to describe a person's history but as a "meaning-giving account," an interpretation of that history as a way of explaining and understanding the participant's action in a classroom (Connelly & Clandinin, 1987, pp. 130-131). Ziegler (1992), a teacher researcher, explains it this way:

> This may include a particular ordering of prior experiences brought to bear on new situations and these orderings bring about new ways of telling stories of who we are and how it is that we are doing what we are doing. This is something I have done as a teacher which has led me to do a dissertation and use narrative as method and mode. One story that I have told was about a student I had in my second year of teaching. As the class was talking about family responsibilities, Felix, a seven year old, had shared about how he helped his family by sweeping the dirt floor each morning. Later that day he was in a group with me reading *The Little White House*, a basal reader about an Anglo family of four who lived in their white house with their dog. Felix looked up at me and asked, "Why is Mother always smiling?" This story has since become an intentional story for me to illustrate how I need to match the material to the child in order to make reading meaningful and relevant. (pp. 14-15)

Ziegler uses a personal narrative to illustrate how she uses narrative to make points about the curriculum to teachers so that they can truly hear her.

Narrative, then, is a technique of interviewing, or listening, that relies on stories. Coles (1989) writes that as a psychiatrist he comes to know patients through their stories. Teachers' stories are part of teachers' lives, and the study of their stories helps us understand the relationship between their lived experiences and their craft knowledge.

This research technique was developed and used initially by teachers of English, who use it with students as well as with one another to understand better the effects of curriculum, the school, and their own teaching. Narratives raise the question of how best to learn from these stories, how to analyze them, and how to keep the speaker's voice intact.

The interest in narrative interview studies is fast growing. See Connelly and Clandinin (1988) and Witherell and Noddings (1991), *Stories Lives Tell: Narrative and Dialogue in Education.*

Structured Interviews

The structured interview is also called a questionnaire-type or directed interview. In this type of qualitative approach, the interviewer asks pre-prepared questions of the participant and controls the direction that an interview takes. Philosophically, structured interviews are very different from ethnographic interviews, and imply certain epistemological differences as well.

To construct such an interview, the interviewer writes down a list of questions and sequences them so that there is a natural flow from one question to another. The wording of these questions should not deviate from interviewee to interviewee. The interviewer tape records or takes careful notes of the responses and later listens to or transcribes the tapes, goes over notes, and expands on them. In a less structured interview format, the interviewer asks the same questions, but does not worry about what order they appear in.

The fixed response is another type of structured interview. Here the interviewer lists the questions on a sheet, asks them of the participant, and then marks off predetermined answers or categories that the answer must fit into. For example:

How important is self-governance to you at the school? (put a check by one):

____ Very important   ____ Important

____ Of little importance   ____ Not important

Another example of a structured interview is when the interviewer asks the participants to talk about a particular experience or event in their lives. "Describe your 6th grade teacher and how she taught math" or, for a teacher, "How do you like having your school be a professional development school?" The researcher maintains control of the interview and directs the interviewees in their answers to questions.

Sociology is probably the original home of this type of interviewing; sources for more information on how to do this include Brady (1979).

Surveys and Questionnaires

A survey or questionnaire shares similarities with the structured interview because the questions are largely predetermined. With surveys and questionnaires, the intent is for the respondents to write answers; the interviewer does not have to be present when they do this. Surveys and questionnaires are a common instrument of practitioner research because they are interviews by proxy and therefore easy to administer, they provide direct responses to factual and attitudinal questions, and they make tabulation and analysis of response almost effortless.

With this kind of research, following a logical sequence of questions is most important, but is often difficult to predict in advance. Questions that appear logical to interviewees are easier for them to answer. Most researchers develop an instrument, then field test or pilot it and revise it before administering it to the specific population.

Initially, the researcher should decide the specific aim of the survey. Is it for an informal assessment or for more formal and external sources? The aim of the survey will help form the specific questions to be investigated and the corresponding sample of participants.

It is important to remember that surveys and questionnaires cannot show causal relationships, but they can indicate associations or correlations. For causal connections, more open-ended interviewing and observations are appropriate. A survey can collect data that will help the researcher see the next step in the research.

Surveys come in two primary types: the descriptive or enumerative kind and the analytic, relational kind. The descriptive kind is similar to a census or public opinion poll, where the questions "how many" or "how often" are asked. The purpose is to count from a representative or class of people; a descriptive survey tells us how many members have a characteristic or how often an event occurs. It is not designed to "explain" anything or to show relationships between A and B.

The analytic survey explores the relationship between variables and is oriented to finding associations and explanations. It is predictive and asks "why" and "what goes with what" kinds of questions. Analytic surveys are usually set up to explore specific hypotheses.

Following is an example from the research notes of an adult education and literacy teacher. Liza Martinez is the coordinator and teacher of a program called Opciones para Mujeres, established to help immigrant women with limited English proficiency. The program uses a bilingual approach; concepts are introduced in Spanish and reinforced with learner-centered and holistic activities in English. Martinez begins the semester with a descriptive survey-registration in-take form:

> As part of the orientation, I had students complete a detailed registration form. This form has a multifold purpose: it has provided me with personal information about the students; it has also helped me to determine whether a student is in need of other social services or should be referred to another educational program, for example. Finally, the registration form also asks students at the end in Spanish what they expect to get from the course. In this way, I have been able to determine whether they are functionally literate in Spanish. If they are not, they can be referred to a Spanish literacy class that is offered. After reviewing each registration form of the present students, I developed a checklist (for analysis) which I divided into several categories. Through the use of simple counting, I compiled the data and came up with a profile of the new group of students. (Martinez, 1993, p. 7)

Martinez collected a great deal of data from her students during the initial meetings. She was then able to use this data to adapt her syllabus for the class and to suggest additional resources for her students. This is also a good example of the action research spiral of plan, act, observe, reflect, and revise.

An example of a practitioner researcher using an analytic-type survey technique involves a middle school teacher, Kathleen Cobb, who used a qualitative research design as a tool to bring forth student perceptions. She asked her students what they thought about their own learning experiences and about how teachers contributed to it:

The main purpose of this study was to hear the students' voices about their own learning and what made it positive in their own eyes. Other studies that have focused on this subject are SooHoo (1991) and Strause (1992).

Initially, a general survey was administrated to 88 eighth graders in a science class. Questions were asked that probed topics such as: what should 8th graders know at the end of the middle school; what do teachers and parents think middle school students should know; affective behavior of teachers that students value; strengths and weaknesses of the student; and perceptions of family members about the student. Next, from this larger group of students, a smaller group of 10 students were invited to participate in a group session to discuss questions about meaningful learning experiences and teachers. These students were chosen to reflect the multicultural characteristics of the school.

The survey was an instrument to give me a general "scan" as to what the students thought about their school experiences relating to subjects they thought important, teachers that had made an impression on them, how their families might influence their perceptions of what was important, and their image of themselves in a school setting. I found that the length of the survey was intimidating to some students as they felt they couldn't or wouldn't complete it fully. Also, more information was gathered than I could analyze in the time period allotted for the completion of this study. I chose to look at the questions that the students had most completely answered and that interested me the most. These questions can be loosely categorized into (a) academic subjects/topics considered to be of importance to the students, (b) elements of the teacher/student relationships that had influenced the students positively or negatively, and (c) situations that they remember as having been the worst or the best in their middle school experience. After studying this particular data from the survey, I decided to concentrate more specifically on the students' learning experiences. I wanted to know what they thought about their experiences. How did they define a good experience? I wanted to know how the students thought the teachers aided in the experience. From the survey, I had learned that good teachers listened, explained, understood, made learning fun, challenged and respected them, and most of all, were characterized as nice. I wanted to know in more detail what made a learning experience meaningful, significant. What was it that a teacher did, in the students' eyes, that made this happen. (Cobb, 1993, pp. 2-3)

This example demonstrates the use of a survey to get a general picture of what students are thinking about their learning experiences. Cobb then interviewed a representative sample of the students to deepen her understanding of what they were saying. After the group interview, she had the students rate different factors that emerged on the surveys as important to a good learning experience. Lastly, she interviewed six of the participating students and focussed on the factors rated highest. She concludes:

I went into this study with a curiosity. What goes on in a middle school student's head as he/she goes about the day? What makes an impression? What will remain in their memories when they are my age looking back on their experiences? As I asked the questions, I became profoundly aware of how students yearn to have someone listen to them, take their reflections seriously, and believe in them. I believe that on some level, most teachers who choose to teach middle school and who enjoy it, know the importance of the student/teacher relationship and its significance to the learning process. It is the power of the students' own words though, that brings this important relationship into focus. There are questions that this study has brought to my attention, and that perhaps, later I can pursue. (Cobb, 1993, p. 10)

The action research spiral worked successfully for Cobb; at this point she is again in the reflective portion of the spiral, perhaps revising her research question in anticipation of future observations and study.

Interview Checklists, Rating Scales, and Inventories

Checklists, rating scales, and inventories all utilize a "closed" type of question; the respondent does not have to write anything down. The response consists of a check or some other indication of choice and the researcher then calculates some kind of score. These techniques are good for administering to groups of students or adults and can easily be returned by dropping them in a box at the school.

Martinez (1993) developed a needs-assessment in-take form. Students were asked to check off as many items as they thought applicable to the following phrase: " I need to improve my English because. . . ."

The responses were then tabulated and the number of people checking each item was placed in parentheses at the end:

- I want to enroll in a vocational or academic class (15)
- I want to speak with people who do not know Spanish (14)
- I want to read books and magazines (14)
- I want to get a job (13)
- I want to speak to a doctor (11)
- I want to read a newspaper (11)
- I want to go shopping (11)
- I want to ask for information (11)
- I want to speak on the telephone (11)
- I want to use public services (10)
- I want to speak with my child's teacher (10)
- I want to speak with coworkers at my job (8)

Martinez used this information to plan and design the class for her students, as well as to ponder the assumptions of previous work that indicated that these types of students were more interested in general educational degree work than in preparing for jobs in the English-speaking community.

Observation

The second core technique in qualitative research is observation. As with interviews, observational research offers many different ways to gather data, and the research question acts as the guide in selecting the best method. The varied ways observation can be done greatly enhance how busy teachers in the classroom can find time to do them. Thus, observation is often the first and most popular form of data gathering for practitioners (see the many examples of using observation in Chapter 3). In this section, we give an overview of observational techniques, then focus on participant observation, checklists, personal action logs and rating scales, mapping material, cultural inventories, and visual techniques such as the use of video and photography.

Observations focus on what is happening in a classroom, a playground, or a hallway, or on what a student or faculty member does in a specific situation over a delimited amount of time. They are best used when the researcher wants to see what is happening in a classroom or playground; they can help demystify what is actually going on as opposed to what one might hope or assume is happening.

Ideally, observations are recorded in a field notebook in as exact a manner as possible, with clear, unbiased language that avoids high-inference descriptors such as nice, pretty, angry, and stylish and focuses on letting words paint a clear picture of the event for the reader. This helps recreate the scene at a later date when the researcher is reviewing notes and needs to understand what happened, not what he or she thought happened. Time constraints for practitioner researchers often mean that a researcher jots a quick observation down in a journal, then later elaborates on it; this works best when the researcher is clear and unbiased in the first jottings.

The basic rules for good observation are:

1. Observe the entire event or incident, called a "stream of behavior."
2. Set clear goals, limitations, and guidelines for the observation.
3. Record observations completely and carefully in a field notebook in an exact manner.

4. Try to be as objective as possible. In other words, strive to be clear and unbiased, and try to recognize when this is not possible.

When an outside researcher begins any observation, as a newcomer he or she will initially try to see as much as possible in order to gain a general understanding of the situation and the observational research possibilities. However, the practitioner researcher already has this general understanding, and it is this enormous amount of tacit knowledge that must be made explicit in order to see it freshly and openly as a researcher. Recording this information as field notes helps this process.

Armed with a general view of the school, and with a particular question, the researcher then begins the process of focusing on a particular situation or stream of behavior. A common mistake at this point is to look only at interesting events or situations. For example, if you are observing in your elementary school classroom and you are watching a reading group led by a student teacher, you might be inclined to record only her encouragement and positive comments to students. If you are more systematic in your observations and listen and record everything the student teacher says and does with each child, you will gain a more inclusive and whole picture of the reading group's dynamics and the student teacher's abilities.

An important point to remember about observations, regardless of where you are observing, is that if an event is truly significant, it will reoccur. If not, then focusing on it to the exclusion of other events will only lead you down a blind alley.

Participant Observation

The first observation technique is participant observation. Its opposite is usually done in a laboratory or experimental environment and implies that the researcher has no contact with the people he or she is observing and is not interested in observing people in their natural surroundings. For practitioner researchers, this is not possible or desirable.

Why is it called participant observation, even if the researcher did not intend to interact with the participants? This term comes from anthropology and refers to the time when anthropologists were called "arm-chair anthropologists." In the late 1800s and into the turn of the century, anthropologists in this new field initially wrote about cultures they never visited; information was culled from documents written by captains of passing ships or from missionaries and colonial administrators who were colonizing a particular culture. Malinowski (1922) was the first anthropologist to conduct fieldwork; his observations of the Trobriand Islanders were later called participant observation because he was there, in the field, rather than home in England in his library reading other people's descriptions of that culture. The term remains, though today we differentiate many varieties of participant observation.

An example of participant observation will provide an idea of the general category. Nihlen (1976) did her research for her dissertation in a 1st grade classroom; the teacher, trying to help her, pinned a sign on her blouse that said "INVISIBLE." This was a big word for the kids, but they caught on and loved the game. Later Nihlen realized that the children never stopped seeing her, but allowed her to watch them as if she was invisible. Nihlen was slowly incorporated into the children's classroom, first by tying shoes and zipping jackets, later with more responsible tasks such as reading to them and participating in the Friday art project. Nihlen tried to be unobtrusive and not a participant, but this was unrealistic; the children helped her become a participant observer. Practitioner researchers usually do not have this problem of choosing their participant stance because of their immersion in the field. Instead, they must struggle with the issue of being more participant than observer. For some practitioners working in larger schools, the role of participant is not taken for granted, nor necessarily welcomed; that poses other problems yet to be understood.

Participant observers have varying degrees of involvement from passive or uninvolved to total and complete participation (see Figure 5.3). Moderate participation means that the researcher tries to maintain a balance between participation and observation. Active participant observers seek to do what the participants in the research scene are doing to understand the process better. Teacher researchers are considered total participant observers, because they are already regular participants in the classroom (Spradley, 1980). However, when

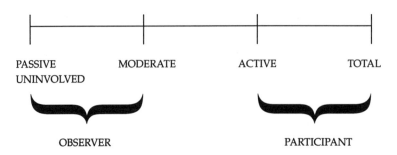

Figure 5.3. Types of Participant Observations

the researcher steps outside his or her role as teacher to study something else in the school, the role changes and he or she is not inherently the total participant observer.

Spradley (1980) does an excellent job of describing the difference between a participant and a participant observer. He discusses such things as crossing the street at the light or getting a cola from a vending machine as examples of tasks we are participants in and have cultural knowledge about. However, this is tacit knowledge after the first few times, and we hardly think about it. Following are Spradley's six major categories of differences between the ordinary participant and the participant observer, differences that are very important for practitioner researchers to remember and work with as they try to do research where they are an everyday participant.

First is the issue of *dual purpose.* A participant observer comes to a situation with two purposes: To engage in activities appropriate in the situation and to observe the activities, people, and physical aspects of the situation. The ordinary participant comes to that same situation with only one purpose: To engage in the appropriate activities.

Second is the issue of *explicit awareness.* Ordinarily, participants in a situation practice selective inattention as a way to escape experiencing overload. If you are in the school cafeteria, you will not pay specific attention to all the children, only those for which you are responsible. You may not closely watch how far or how close each child stands from another in a given line, and you may not closely observe how they make their selection of food. You have unconsciously selected certain stimuli to be more aware of, and some to be less aware of. However, if you are a researcher interested in line-standing behavior of children, you will watch the spaces between children as well as a host of other things. (And, of course, there is the issue of how to explain your presence in the lunch line when it is not your turn to work in the cafeteria. This gets into the issue some practitioner researchers have discussed concerning what it means when you turn up in your school where you are not "normally" expected to be. This creates problems of role definition.)

Third is the issue of a *wide-angle lens*. At the same time the participant observer is selecting things in the environment that do not warrant attention, he or she is using a wide-angle lens to conduct observations. As a staff member in a school, you may not have lunchroom duty, but if you are studying line-standing behavior of children that is one place you will want to go. You will try to observe everything about the lines that is occurring: distance and closeness of children, straight versus crooked lines, shoving and pushing, hugging, voices of children and of adults, and any other behaviors that may occur.

Fourth is the *insider-outsider experience*. Practitioner researchers interact in various activities at their schools. They are insiders; this gives the activities a meaning and coherence understood to insiders. Participant observers need to be both insiders and outsiders simultaneously. As a teacher, you are an insider in your classroom. As a researcher, you try to be an outsider and view yourself and the classroom as a stranger would. This will help you understand the unspoken and hidden curriculum in the classroom. You are also an outsider to many settings within the school and must adapt and understand your multiple roles as a researcher and help others to adapt to this changing situation.

Fifth is the issue of *introspection*. In observational research, the researcher becomes the research tool, and must constantly analyze his or her own feelings and subjective reactions to this role. A participant observer can take nothing for granted, and an introspective and reflective stance helps gain perspective on events. This also helps the researcher understand new and old situations and gain skill in learning the rules of the cultural scene.

The sixth issue is one of *record keeping*. A participant observer needs to keep a detailed record of events he or she observes. Sometimes teachers cannot do this at the time; then it is important to jot down a key word or words that will help jar the memory later when the researcher can write down a more comprehensive record. The longer one waits to record an event, the harder it is to recreate an accurate picture. Many teacher researchers use an open notebook on their desks in which they make passing comments as they work with children. Others jot down things while children are involved in group activities, or when another adult is working with the class.

We offer here the traditional format of using one side of the notebook page for observations, and the other side for personal feelings, comments, and hunches. We have already discussed the importance of keeping observations and feelings separate. But is this really a useful way to record data? Following is an example from a practitioner researcher. Judith Pearson, a kindergarten teacher, tried to develop a way to observe three children who were identified as behavior problems; the traditional ways were not helping her.

Why did I choose to observe three children? I needed to start somewhere, and if my basic question had to do with behavior management, observing behavior seemed a logical place to begin. It also gave me an entry point at which to try changing my focus of the classroom, having been fascinated with Spindler's [1982] and Erickson's [1973] ethnographic principle of "making the familiar strange." If I understood better how children thought, would I more easily be able to change my reality of how I saw them? If I understood the child's reality, would my idea of how to manage their behavior change? The child learns early on how to say what adults want to hear—a form of translation competence, I suppose, on the part of the child. Spradley defines it as "the ability to translate the meanings of one culture into a form that is appropriate to another culture" (Spradley, 1979, p. 19). I am attempting to see their culture sans the translation.

Although I began with observations of three boys, the pursuit invariably led to observation of myself, teetering back and forth as I attempted to make sense out of what I saw and said and did. I am still, at this writing, struggling to comprehend what I've seen and heard this semester.

As I began my observations, I realized that I had not yet learned the "tricks of the trade." Time and energy restraints constantly plagued me. I began taking notes on what I saw. I found that I was writing all the time instead of interacting with the children. Although I'd plan to have time in the afternoon where others could take over (the classroom), it rarely worked out. Like the day I had planned to finish the sociograms. It seemed simple. I would do them after quickly helping the children put together our cookie recipe that had to chill. With my teacher's aide in the room I would have the rest of the hour. Ha! One interruption after the other delayed the cookie making and I ended up with no time at all. Next, I went to PE class. This was a perfect place to observe since the children didn't run to me. However, even knowing this, I wasn't willing or able to get away again for this kind of observation.

Whenever I could I took notes during class, but even as fast as I wrote, I wasn't using nearly enough detail; the words did not come swiftly to me and the event was over before I could record it accurately. Also, using a notebook was clumsy and it got lost easily, as I'd set it somewhere when things needed attending to.

The next problem was getting a recording system that worked for me. I tried a divided notebook but it was too awkward to carry around. So I went to a legal pad. I could usually find one of these and I could easily whisk the pages into a notebook. I'd write observations only on one side, saving the other side for my own thoughts. The system still lacks easy and quick use and access. Trying to solve this problem has given me a new insight into myself. I always thought of myself as organized, even though I have trouble remembering which organized file something is in. I think there are levels of being organized, something like the levels of thinking skills. I'm still at the factual level. I'm obsessed with doing it, but haven't the understanding of it yet.

So, I abandoned the notetaking and turned to the video camera. I planted it on a tripod and got what I got, which wasn't always my three boys. Nevertheless, it was surprisingly revealing. Every taped session had interesting interactions. I found the drawbacks to be: (a) finding a convenient place for the tripod where the children wouldn't trip over it, (b) placing it where I could see the whole scene, yet still be close enough to get the scene's voices, (c) taking the time to transcribe (each tape took 4 to 6 home viewing hours). I ended up with countless pages of observations but I wasn't sure how to abstract from them for data. My first idea was to use them to form a profile of one boy, which I did. (Pearson, 1993, p. 6)

This is a good example of a practitioner researcher trying to work within a traditional framework of qualitative research to conduct research, then adapting various methods to the reality of her site. When she has trouble reproducing the traditional technique, she concludes that she is not organized or does not know the "tricks of the trade," when in reality she needs more realistic and usable research techniques that take into account the frenzied pace of her day.

Another kind of participant observation was developed by a practitioner researcher at Emerson Elementary School. Geraldine Garcia, a Title V academic tutor for Native American students, did a series of critical environmental observations. She had a tiny room to meet with students, more like an enlarged closet than a real room. When Native American children were identified by their regular teachers as needing help in subjects such as reading, math, and social studies, they were sent to Garcia for a half-hour each day. At any given time, she had up to six students, each needing help in a different academic area. She worked with whatever assignments the children brought to her from their homeroom teachers.

When Garcia began teaching at Emerson, she was not aware of its professional development program. She enrolled in an on-site teacher researcher course:

I was surprised and pleased to discover that a university class was to be offered on-site as part of the professional development for the staff. I read with interest the initial articles about qualitative research and thought about how it would be relevant in my room. The research coursework and the discussions with the other teachers provided an opportunity to look critically at my room and I decided to change the environment. At the same time I began to realize that this transformation of space to enhance learning provided a unique source of research data. I recorded data by drawing pictures and writing descriptively about each stage of the changes and what process I went through in order to see the room as a place I could manipulate to enhance learning. I moved furniture, pushed back bulletin boards, and utilized a refrigerator, which was in the room, as a place for magnetized letters of the alphabet. (Garcia, 1991, p. 10)

Garcia developed a method that combined mapping and observation. Each week she made a picture of the room and wrote descriptive field notes. When she changed something in the room, she noted the children's as well as her own responses to the change. This way each change helped promote a new change, in the curriculum as well as in the physical structure of the room. At each juncture, she explained to the research class both her own transformation and the changes in the classroom. They were able to give her encouragement as well as additional suggestions. Garcia speaks about her classroom environment:

Within that week I looked at my environment carefully and tried to find ways to enhance learning. I started rearranging the furniture so it would not be cluttered and crammed like before. In the arrangement I noticed how the students were eager to use the chalkboard. The students would be trying to squeeze on both sides of the table to get to the board. After rearranging the furniture, the students noticed the blackboard space. There was more room to walk around the table. Their eyes just beamed when they saw the space. "Wow, you changed the room." "It looks nice in here." "Now we can have a place to use the blackboard." The environment made a difference in the way the children developed work and play. The students used the blackboard for doing math problems. It invited other students to join them. It was exciting to see the students being excited about learning and sharing. The blackboard also created the freedom to draw and explore one's ability. (Garcia, 1991, p. 46)

Garcia reports that she grew professionally as well as personally in the process of researching and implementing change in her classroom. Of the research class and her work in it, Garcia says that it "has brought about great sparks and challenges. The class has created a spiraling effect in the way I view learning and environment within myself and the Title V program. We as educators need to take time and become aware of the things around us and learn from our students" (Garcia, 1991, p. 46).

Personal Action Logs,
Checklists, and Rating Scales

We have already discussed how to use checklists and rating scales in conducting interviews; the same principles are true when conducting observations and using forms that are developed prior to the research activity. Personal action logs, checklists, and rating scales represent structured aids to direct observation and are most useful when the researcher knows that certain conditions and events will be present. These tools indicate when certain behaviors are present, but do not give information about range or quality of the behavior. They are most useful for confirmation and when triangulated with other forms of observation and interviewing.

Personal action logs are prewritten record sheets that document a practitioner researcher's activities, or that of a colleague, in his or her own classroom or school office. They record the bare essentials of human behavior and are most useful when kept over a length of time along with more extensive field notes, interviews, and the like (Kemmis & McTaggart, 1982; Walker, 1985). For example, you might use a personal action log to keep a running record of the activities of the Chapter 1 Reading Program teacher. You would ask the teacher to jot down every 15 minutes or so what he is doing at that moment. Sometimes it will be impossible to make a notation; then the teacher must try to reconstruct the event later or leave it blank. The log would stand as vivid testimony to how busy the teacher is, data in itself. At the end of the month you both would have a very good idea about exactly what kinds of activities the teacher performed each day. This, coupled with interviews and other kinds of data, would provide a very good picture of the teacher's work in the school.

Logs may be kept in a chart summary form or in a more narrative form, which verges on the boundaries of a diary, discussed later in this chapter. Either way, the researcher must decide beforehand on an arbitrary length of time between entries and keep to that time frame as much as possible. This way not only "interesting" events are recorded, and the researcher gets a more accurate sequencing of daily activities.

The *checklist* focuses the observer's attention on certain behaviors and allows a quick tallying of the presence, absence, or frequency of occurrence. Points must be observed in the sequence in which they occur. McKernan (1991) enumerates four details to include in developing a school-based checklist:

1. Points to be observed are listed in their actual sequence of happening.
2. All similar traits/attributes are included in categories.
3. All the relevant and specific points are listed.
4. Space is provided for tallying marks on the form itself so that analysis is eased.

See Figure 5.4 for two examples of checklists.

Rating scales for observations are constructed to make evaluations of human behavior and activity. The researcher places an object, person, or idea along a sequential scale in terms of estimated value. The participant is asked to assess, along the continuum, some characteristic from high to low, never to always, or the like. These scales can be used by researchers to gather data about such things as curriculum, teacher-initiated activities, and discussion times, and to create evaluation scales of performance of self or students (see Figure 5.5, Examples 1 and 2).

Example 1

Student participation

_____ Participates eagerly

_____ Contributes to group

_____ Follows speakers or activity with eyes, but quiet

_____ Does not watch or participate

_____ Displays disruptive behaviors

Student involvement in play

_____ Dominates playmates

_____ Shares and/or cooperates

_____ Goes along with majority rule

_____ Disruptive

_____ Does not play with others

Example 2

Checklist of Student Teacher Skills

Behavior	Skill Observed	
	Yes	No
1. Indicates lesson objectives?	_____	_____
2. Is systematic?	_____	_____
3. Uses audio/visual aids correctly?	_____	_____
4. Gains and holds students' attention?	_____	_____
5. Displays enthusiasm?	_____	_____
6. Speech is understandable, audible?	_____	_____
7. Students appear involved?	_____	_____
8. Good management skills?	_____	_____

Figure 5.4. Examples of Types of Checklists for Observers

Another type of rating scale is the *numerical rating scale*. This is the simplest to construct and analyze; it is usually numbered from 1 to 5, but can go up to 10 or more. A mean score for a person or student can be derived by adding up the number value of each item and dividing it by the number of items used. When rating a group, the number value for each item should be calculated and divided by the number of persons completing it. These mean scores act as an important index of affect and belief (see Figure 5.5, Example 3).

Graphic rating scales are the most widely used type of rating scales. In this format, the rater places a mark along a clearly defined line or continuum that may include numbers (see Figure 5.5, Examples 4 and 5).

Mapping

Another tool in the category of observations is mapping. Mapping has long been used in the study of proxemics, which is the development of categories of distances that people place between each other (Hall, 1974). Mapping is most useful for doing quick observations in a classroom or playground that lead to plentiful data.

The technique involves using graph paper and making an exact map to scale of the scene in question. A classroom is an easy example: The researcher can do the measuring when the room is empty, or let the kids help and make it a lesson in measurement. If the room has old floor tiles, many are 1-inch square and need only to be counted. If not, the floor should be measured with tape. The outside walls should be measured first, then doors and windows should be marked on the map, other objects that are permanent along the walls should be marked, and finally the furniture should be marked. Many researchers designate immovable furniture, rarely moved furniture, and regularly moved furniture such as student desks, chairs, and tables. Each should be carefully recorded and drawn on the graph paper.

One middle school teacher researcher made a map of the floor plan including the permanent and rarely moved objects. Each week she recorded where the student desks were; she then compared these maps after several months and learned a lot about student preferences for shape of desk areas when they were combined, who wanted to be next to whom, and how separate the girls and boys wanted to be. She was startled to find that all students wanted to be closer to her in the front of the room, and that the boys actually got closer.

A map can help chart adult movement in the classroom. You, as the site researcher, can create the map and you and a colleague can

Example 1

To what extent do you as a student participate in the discussion?
_____ Never
_____ Seldom
_____ Occasionally
_____ Frequently
_____ Always

Example 2

How would rate this new unit on rediscovering Columbus?
_____ Extremely imaginative
_____ Very imaginative
_____ Imaginative
_____ Very unimaginative
_____ Extremely unimaginative

Example 3

To what extent does the student participate in the discussions?
_____ 0. never
_____ 1. seldom
_____ 2. occasionally
_____ 3. frequently
_____ 4. always

Example 4

The aims of this project are:

1	2	3	4	5
very clear				very unclear

Example 5

To what extent does the student participate in small groups?

(always)	(frequently)	(occasionally)	(seldom)	(never)
X				
4	3	2	1	0

Example 6

Interviews make me:

extremely anxious	very anxious	anxious	somewhat anxious	not at all anxious

Figure 5.5. Types of Interview Rating Scales

chart each other. For example, one elementary school teacher charted a colleague every 2 minutes for half-an-hour over several weeks. He put a number on the map where the teacher was standing at that moment. This helped the teacher see how she utilized her room and which children got more attention through simple proximity.

Another use of maps is for proxemic studies more elaborate than the above example. Staples (1993) studied a student teacher during the student teacher's initial student teaching and the first 2 years of his own classroom. She drew the classroom maps and was able to see a change in his proxemics during the course of the 2½-year study.

Hall's proxemic categories (1966, 1974) range from closer than 6 inches to 25 feet and beyond. The four categories are intimate, personal, social, and public. Hall bases these four categories on manifestations of territoriality in both animals and humans. Staples (1993) feels that the kinds of interactions that occur within each category are culturally influenced. An examination of the proxemics between, the teacher, Bob, and his students provided information "about the implicit culture in his classroom and how it changed over time" (Staples, 1993, p. 37). Following is a brief description of how Staples collected her data:

> Each time I observed in the classroom, I began with a half hour of recording proxemic data. I used six copies of a scale floor plan to plot at 5-minute intervals the location of all people in the classroom, identifying the adults and noting the sex of each student. Any verbal interaction was noted with arrows showing who was addressing whom. This was done in a sequenced sweep of predetermined sections of the classroom. Each observation session resulted in six samples of interaction behavior that, taken together, was reasonably representative of the pattern during that session. Using a home constructed stamp with proxemic boundary lines as radiating circles on it, I centered and pressed the inked stamp over the adult symbols on the maps. I used a large hat pin that slipped through the center of the stamp to stick into the center of the symbol on the map and guide the stamp down. The stamp was constructed to match the scale of the floor plan map. Then the number of student symbols

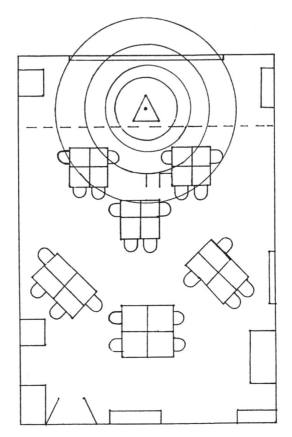

Figure 5.6. Mapping Examples—Staples

in each proxemic category surrounding the adult was counted and recorded (see Figure 5.6). This information was used to chart over time the teacher and student interaction patterns with a large group of students such as the whole class, with a small group of students, and with a single student. (Staples, 1993, p. 37)

To accomplish something this ambitious and informative, a practitioner researcher will probably need to work with a colleague and trade mapping activities. Many teachers train student teachers to become practitioner researchers as they begin teaching. This enables them to reflect on their practice and develop ways to study their own teaching.

Following is an example from the journal of a kindergarten teacher who tried to using mapping to gather data:

> My plan was: check every three minutes to see where children were, what they were doing, and with whom they were playing. At first I tried to chart everyone. I found that it was very difficult to keep track of who was where and to maintain a systematic span. They moved and changed groups too fast. So I disregarded the time intervals and tried to note groupings, placements and interactions. Still it was too much. I couldn't keep track of all the children along with doing my playground duties.
>
> Some problems interfere with this observation method: (a) The children's needs and my supervisory duties, (b) the windy weather, making note-taking awkward at best, (c) infrequent recess duty—only twice a week. The other days I would try to get outside, but so many other things got in the way, not the least of them being a need for a breather. Nevertheless, I feel this type of record keeping would be valuable with as much time as I could manage. If I concentrated on only four children a week, I wouldn't be so overwhelmed. That way I would be tracking each child every six weeks or so, giving me a pretty good picture of that child's patterns.
>
> I started observations of classroom play and interaction during Choice Time. I didn't get very far with this, finding it so hard to sacrifice the time it took away from my personal interactions with the children. Moreover, I didn't discover an easy system for recording the data. First I made a map of the classroom, intending to write children's names directly on the map. It took too much time to find the location on the map. So I numbered the locations, intending to write the location number after the child's name—it took too much

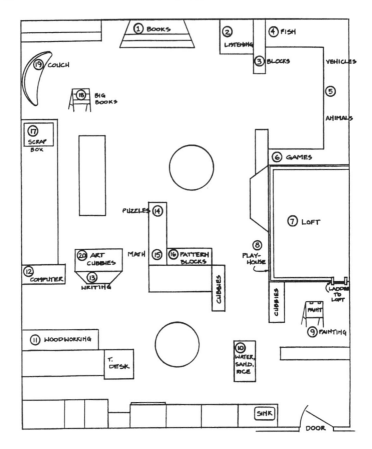

Figure 5.7. Mapping Examples—Pearson

time to find the number and transfer it to the name (see Figure 5.7). Finally, I made an alphabetized list of all the possible Choice Time activities and wrote the abbreviated child's name after the location. This worked the best. I think that if I combine the playground and classroom observation, doing only four children a week, it might be workable. I made up a data sheet that would work for both indoors and outdoors to keep track of the four children observed, their choice of companions, and their choice of playing place. (Pearson, 1993, p. 22)

This example places the struggles of the practitioner trying to conduct research in her own classroom at the center of the question of which techniques are most useful.

Material Culture Inventories

Material inventories of a culture were a standard technique used by early anthropologists in their attempts to understand the tools and art of different cultures. Today educational anthropologists use them in the classroom and school to record how people move and change their environment.

In conducting such an inventory, the researcher should carefully mark the boundary of observations and inventory. A classroom, hallway, entryway, or the lavatory graffiti can be selected. The researcher must decide how frequently he or she will observe and record data, and how he or she will describe its placement.

Staples (1993) made systematic and detailed notes of the material contents of her teacher/participant's room and referenced them to the maps she had made of the floor, ceiling, and walls. She writes that her notes

included everything from soda pop cans to books to computer disks. Documents such as schedules and memos which he had affixed to the wall, bulletin board displays made either by him or the students, displayed student work, posters with class rules—all comprised material for analysis and were a special category in the material inventory. This material was integrated with the behavior recorded in field observations and with interviews with the teacher. Issues examined were how the behavioral and material systems of communication in the classroom interrelated. Photographs were also taken as a supplementary source. (pp. 40-41)

Staples redid the material inventory every 3 months and gained valuable information on the changing material culture of the classroom.

McKernan (1988) noted the amount of political graffiti found on school desks as an indicator of political socialization reflecting political allegiances in Northern Irish secondary schools. LeCompte (1969) conducted a study of nonattendance at school and the amount of broken glass littering the school grounds. When the glass was removed and local shops shifted from selling bottles to selling cans, school attendance increased.

Visual Recordings and Photography

A final technique of observation is visual recordings. Photography and videotaping are excellent ways for practitioner researchers to record data from situations in which they are also participants. The practitioner researcher takes off his or her hat as participant and puts on the researcher hat and analyzes the data at his or her leisure.

The camera acts as an extension of our senses; it records not only what we want it to see, but all the surroundings as well. The camera has been used since its invention as a clarifier and a modifier of ecological and human understanding. As a precise recorder of reality, it can turn raw circumstances into data (Collier, 1967). Margaret Mead and Gregory Bateson were the first to use photography as part of research in anthropology (see Bateson & Mead, 1942), and Mead continued to use photography in her work in child development.

In the last 20 years, educational anthropologists have begun to use video to analyze discrete events in the classroom. Gearing and Sangree (1979) delineate aspects of cultural transmission in the classroom; they also work with teacher researchers in this area. Erickson (1986) labels his video analysis in the classroom "microethnography."

With the movement of VCRs into schools and homes, the use of videotaping a classroom has increased enormously. Teachers or counselors can run the video camera themselves in their rooms, or get a camera person to help. The video camera can be focused on a small group activity so that the teacher can participate in the activity, or another person can scan the room, moving the camera slowly from one end to the other and back again over a period of time. The teacher can do timed observations of certain segments of the room. The list is endless and the camera will follow the researcher's imagination.

If you decide to videotape your room, test the camera and your tape before starting. If you use a microphone, make sure it can pick up the group or activity you want or consider using an additional

1. What do you wish to observe?
2. What are the features of the event?
3. Are the goals of the lesson clear?
4. What is the role of the teacher?
5. Are students involved/interested?
6. Who is doing the talking?
7. What type of utterances are made?
8. What type of questions are asked (convergent/divergent)?
9. What type of pupil involvement is there?
10. What is the pace?
11. What style of classroom/pupil organization is used?
12. What negative features of this performance present themselves?
13. What nonverbal behavior is present?
14. Are the voices clear?
15. Is the language formal/informal?
16. What mannerisms are evident?
17. Do any distractions occur?
18. What things have you learned from this analysis?

Figure 5.8. Checklist for Video Camera Use and Analysis

microphone. Slow, steady camera moves are most effective; fast moves make for difficult viewing.

Children are accustomed to the video camera and the VCR; some have them in their own homes and all have seen them at school and in their lives. What becomes irresistible to them is that one is now in their classroom looking at them. The researcher needs to "habituate" students to the camera; letting it run for a few days before beginning to tape will normalize it for the students and enhance data gathering in a naturalistic setting. The researcher should find out the district's policies on videotaping children, even for personal use. Figure 5.8 is a checklist for video camera use and analysis in the classroom.

A videotape provides a comprehensive record that is reliable and accurate, that can be viewed and analyzed later, and that can be used as exemplars for demonstration to students and other staff. However, its disadvantages include the difficulty of transcription, the need for expensive equipment that a school district may not have, and the possible distortion of aiming the camera only at certain things.

Elliott (1991) suggests that researchers review the entire tape initially, stopping at insightful events and carefully marking them using the numbering system on the VCR. Then they should transcribe, loosely or precisely depending on the intended use, the relevant events for the research question. Transcribing videotapes by hand is a time-consuming and exhausting job, though well worth the effort. Walker (1985) states that videotaping has made it possible to solve such problems as interrater reliability, selectivity, and validity; however, we are now burdened with such issues as intrusiveness or reactivity of this technology on the setting.

McKernan (1991) uses videotapes of "teachers engaged in discussion work and the implementation of new curriculum materials with interested schools wishing to adopt a new discussion approach shown in the tapes in life skills coursework" (p. 105).

Examples from practitioner researcher's journals and research reports indicate that videotaping is seen as an extremely useful tool; it is fairly easy and less stressful to collect data this way, and one can find the time later to index and analyze the footage. Following is an excerpt from a study of surface and hidden curriculum in a science class for 6th graders:

> This is my first attempt at an in-depth look at my teaching. I am searching specifically for insights into how I am attending to the various aspects of the politics of the learning experiences I provide for my students. This is a first experience with participatory research. It was an exercise in "making the road as I was walking" (Horton et al., 1990).
>
> The data for this investigation was taken from a video of a lesson on germinating seeds. The students are 6th graders in my class who are with me for a three period block each day. I am responsible for teaching science, math and Spanish to these students. My primary focus in all I undertake to teach is to provide opportunities to use language, the language of science (or math or Spanish) in the four domains of literacy.
>
> Before I began to analyze the video of this class I wanted to look at social interactions between the students and myself. I wanted to look at the complexity of the material I was

> asking them to spend time on. I wanted to see if I could get
> any insight into what the students thought about their learn-
> ing. I began by looking at the video with the students, because
> they asked to see it on the day it was filmed. They were given
> the option to respond in writing about what they saw. (Ortega,
> 1993, p. 20)

Ortega used this videotape to reflect on her presentation of curriculum as a teacher, as well as to show the students their behavior in
class and to have them reflect on their work in the room. As an action
researcher, she was able to revise the curriculum and then move ahead.
This also became part of a larger study she conducted for a practitioner research class.

Still photography is an interesting and exciting way to capture
data in a classroom or school building; its primary advantage is that
it is a quick and inexpensive method of recording data. Photos document artifacts and behaviors and offer a window into the school and
its events. Walker (1985) argues that nonpractitioner "educational
researchers tend not to treat schools and classrooms as culturally exotic
or indeed as problematic settings" (p. 100) in which the use of photography would greatly enhance the research project and data collection. Thus, they do not consider photographing this environment.

Walker and Weidel (1985) used photography to collect evidence
of children' experiences in a London secondary school. They photo-
graphed a range of subjects during the academic year. The project,
"Pictures: A Collaborative Project (1977-1979)," was placed in an
exhibition with teacher and pupil interpretive comments juxtaposed.
It was also used as a basis of discussion between teachers and students
in the math department, and for an evening meeting with parents.

Permission must usually be obtained to photograph children
and adults in the school, particularly if used outside of personal
research. The researcher should check with the district and school.

Archives and Documents

This section examines the various kinds of archival approaches
and document searches available to the practitioner researcher.

Archival refers primarily to historical research, and is the process of critical inquiry into past events to produce an accurate description and interpretation of those events and their meaning.

There are two major sources of information in history. One is the primary source, which is an original or first-hand account of events such as personal diaries, letters, and official records such as census materials, school board minutes, policies, and legislative actions. Secondary materials are at least once removed from the event itself. Newspaper accounts are a good example of this category of material.

Primary sources should be used for research whenever possible. All sources must be externally authenticated to evaluate the validity of the document to ensure that a document was written by whom and when it states. In addition, internal criticism helps evaluate the meaning, accuracy, and trustworthiness of the content of the document. For example, was the author of a letter sent from the battlefield predisposed to present a biased rather than objective account of the actual battle? People have a tendency to color writings, to write more figuratively than accurately, and, at times, to borrow heavily from others. The researcher's job, if using personal documents, is to try to understand what was actually going on.

A single document can rarely stand on its own. Part of examining history is to cross-reference several documents before accepting a statement as fact. The researcher should evaluate each document in its chronological position and in light of comments that precede it, not comments that appeared later.

The goal is to synthesize the information available from as many different sources as possible. Try to use differing types of information such as statistics, school board records, newspapers, diaries, and personal letters—anything that will add context to the situation under study. Pull the central ideas together, see the possible continuity between and among them, and formulate additional hypotheses or revise the initial ones.

History is usually reported and written in a narrative form; it can provide an educator with a broad perspective about educational issues and problems. It can assist in understanding why things are as they are. Educational reform and social reform are functions often served by historical research. We are better equipped to predict and move into the future by knowing our past, which can perhaps help us avoid mistakes already committed.

One example of how archival techniques and document searches are combined with oral history is in the Emerson Elementary School Oral History Project. As the researchers interviewed the staff about the last 5 years at Emerson, older staff also discussed the earlier years at the school. This necessitated a search for school board records mentioning Emerson or professional development schools, newspaper articles on the school and public reaction, and school attendance records. The researchers sought primary sources when they could, and accepted secondary sources such as the local newspaper's mention of a document when they had no choice. They also sought personal documents such as diaries and journals written by early staff and parent participants in the school. These were combined with oral history interviews to broaden the view of the school and community and to help triangulate. The varied sources kept all of the researchers involved in this project from assuming their reality as the only reality of the experience of Emerson Elementary School.

For a good discussion of historiography, see Tuchman (1994).

Journals and Diaries

The development in education of the diary and journal as research tools and as data has occurred primarily through teachers of English. Journals are personal documents that can also be used as a research tool to capture reflections and encounters; see Ballenger, 1993; Christman et al., in press; and Richards, 1989. Also see Chapter 3 for examples. Journals can also promote educational objectives when used between teachers and students in the classroom (see SooHoo, 1991, as discussed in Chapter 3) and encourages description, interpretation, and reflection on the part of the teacher as well as the student.

The journal acts as a narrative technique and records events, thoughts, and feelings that have importance for the writer. As a record kept by a student, it can inform the teacher researcher about changing thoughts and new ideas and the progression of learning. McKernan (1991) lists three types of traditional diaries or journals:

1. The intimate journal, which is extremely personal and full of personal sentiments, confessions, and a log of events as seen through the individual eyes of the writer. An intimate journal is written in almost every day.
2. The memoir, which is a more impersonal document, written in less often, and aspires to be more objective and not concentrated on personal feelings. The records of war correspondents are good examples, as is the diary of Anne Frank (1952).
3. The log, which is more of a running record of events, such as a list of meetings attended and calls made.

Practitioner researchers, particularly teachers of English, have been using journals as a way to communicate more intimately with students for a long time. As an evaluation tool, journals can inform the researcher about his or her teaching as no other method can, and allow a teacher to implement curricular changes rapidly. Journals also increase writing and communication skills with students.

The journal/diary can be kept by practitioner researchers to document the classroom or school and can also be used as a personal case history. It can be used by students to increase writing and communication skills and to evaluate both the teacher and the curriculum.

The keeping of a journal/diary encourages a reflective stance on the part of the writer, and can provide a rich source of data on the daily life of a classroom.

Cazden, Diamondstone, and Naso (1988) report that the results of teacher research on writing can help teachers "recalibrate" their pedagogy and their own understanding of their work. Thus, the work of practitioner researchers using journal writing benefits both the students and the teachers.

Raisch (1992) writes about secondary student teachers and their cooperating teachers becoming teacher-researchers; she used journal writing among each group and among herself and the teachers extensively. She found the most difficult part was in the analysis of the data, and ended up coding for themes within the journals in order to guarantee participant voice.

Studies by teachers using journals and diaries increase daily. See Fulwiler (1987), Goswami and Stillman (1987), and Miller (1990) for exciting work by teacher researchers using diaries and journals.

Analysis

Ongoing Analysis and Reflection

When you begin to develop your study it is very important to recognize that at various intervals you must stop gathering data and reflect on what you have thus far. For example, if you are doing observations of teacher proxemics in the classroom using a mapping technique, after a few weeks you may want to stop gathering data until you have had a chance to look at the maps.

The first thing you need to know is whether your question still seems answerable and worth asking. Then you need to check to see if the techniques you began with are gathering what you want as far as data are concerned; that is, are they catching the particular kinds of data you want and filtering out data that are not relevant at this time?

Once you have answered the first two questions, you can begin to look analytically at the data for a preliminary review. For example, if you were following student movement around the teacher in the classroom and wanted to know how many students hung around the teacher and by what gender and ethnicity, then you should have recorded student position and included gender and ethnicity or name (so that you could fill in the demographics later). You could then begin to count up the number of students in each category who were close or distant from the teacher.

Next you can ask the question, "Do I need more of the same data, or can I change what I am doing and, perhaps, look at my own movements?" Depending on the question and what data you need to refine it and provide answers, you can begin to develop other data-gathering strategies. One problem that frequently develops for practitioner researchers is the dilemma of not enough time and the practicality of the data-gathering techniques themselves. A technique to gather proxemic data might be impossible to implement in your site; if so, it would be time to regroup and figure out another strategy for collecting data.

If you are gathering data over a long period of time, such as a school year, every 2 months or so you need to stop and see what you are collecting, how it relates to the research question, and how efficient it is for you to gather data in this way. This is also a good time to see if you can begin to triangulate some of the various forms of data, such as interviews and observations, and see if there are discrepancies that you will want to explore further.

Stopping periodically in the data-collection process also allows you to see if you have any gaps in the data, holes where you need data to answer the questions. Seeing this early on in the research allows you to develop the correct techniques and questions for a complete study.

In qualitative research, the research question often changes over time. When you begin, you have a general idea of the question and focus of your initial data collection. With time you might see things differently, and the data might lead you down multiple paths. There is no problem with this shifting focus if you feel comfortable with it and are working alone or with like-minded colleagues. However, if it is not feasible or comfortable to modify and change the focus, then you need to keep redirecting your inquiry toward answering the initial research question. Frequent pauses in the data collection for analysis serve this goal nicely.

We discussed the issues of reliability and validity in Chapter 2 and will not go into them again in this section. Suffice it to say that qualitative research in general, and action research in particular, use differing kinds of checks for their data that encourage application of ongoing discoveries in the research, as well as reflection on the data.

The Final Analysis

When is enough data enough to end the research? Usually when you run out of time, finances, or, more appropriately, when you begin to see duplications and repeats in the data. The ending point can also reflect the action research spiral of planning, acting, observing, reflecting, and revising. If you have studied your site sufficiently and have changed curriculum or structure, and your research work is paying off in your role of teacher or principal, then you may choose to stop. This section is for those who wish to continue with the analysis of their data.

If you have collected data over a school year or throughout an entire year, then you have a large amount of notes, interviews, maps, observations, and the like with which to work. You have periodically stopped data collection and reviewed where you are going, perhaps going forward in a straight line or perhaps changing direction to answer the question better. You have filled in gaps in data to create the most holistic picture you can. You have a good start on the final analysis of the data.

The first step is to put all your data together, reread your initial question, and then reread all your data, starting with observations and then going to field notes, your journal, and interviews. Wander through the data, making notes of items that strike you.

A comprehensive scanning of all the data in one or two long sittings will provide some emerging patterns with which to begin the process of analysis. Take these initial emergent patterns and see what fits together, what converges. It is here that you begin to match, contrast, and compare the patterns or constructs in the data in earnest. Hunches or intuitive leaps are very important and usually extremely significant in the process of analysis and should not be ignored.

Various conceptual techniques are useful in pouring over the data. LeCompte and Preissle (1993) outline them, as do Lincoln and Guba (1985) and Patton (1980). Here we present some of the most useful techniques along with some examples of how they can be applied.

Initially, everything you have collected is interesting. Your job is to code data into initial constructs or aggregates of data and compare them to each other to see if they really are separate circles of information or if they can be placed together. Keep doing this with your initial categories, and keep comparing and contrasting them. Examine how frequently they occur and in what order.

Developing Coding Categories

Developing coding systems for your data is of paramount importance. Coding systems enable you to see categories emerge from the data; consequently the data become more manageable. Differing research questions generate varying categories; every question needs some organization to address the data for answers.

Qualitative research data is messy and comes in large containers. It lacks the slim portfolio of numbers. This is all the more reason to come to grips with notebooks full of observational data and boxes full of tapes and transcriptions. Earlier we suggested reading over all the data collected and refreshing yourself with the initial question. Next you will need to begin separating and isolating potentially interesting and important data. Remember, as you go along and develop codes or categories, you will always be cross-checking yourself to make sure the data are speaking louder than the researcher. Allow yourself to see if the data can fit into some categories; develop or use existing codes and see if the data fit. If they do not, no harm has been done, and you can try another angle. The more perspectives you gain on the data, the more you learn about it.

Following is a brief description of a "family of codes" that might suggest ways coding can be accomplished. They are based on the codes suggested by Bogdan and Biklen (1982).

Setting/Context Codes

Setting/context codes are fairly easy codes, and encompass the large context of a study. Descriptive literature on the site goes here, as do newspaper articles. General descriptions by the participants, as well as descriptive statistics, fit here.

Situation Codes

Place data here that tell how the participants define the setting or particular topics. This is where participants' thoughts on their worldview and how they see themselves are placed. If you have various participants, such as students, principals, and support staff, you might want to have a code for each one. "Some 'definitions of the situation' codes in a study of women's perceptions of their own elementary school experiences included 'feminist awareness,' 'image of present self,' and 'influences on interpreting past'" (Biklen, 1973).

Perspectives Held by Participants

This includes codes for shared rules and norms as well as general points of view that are a little more specific than above. Sometimes these perspectives are captured in particular phrases people use.

Participants' Ways of Thinking About People and Objects

These codes represent what participants think of each other and their understanding of one another and the objects that make up their world. Teachers' views about the nature of the students they teach is an example.

Process Codes

Process codes refer to words and phrases that facilitate organizing sequences of events, changes over time, and passages from one type or kind of status to another. To use this code you must view people over a period of time and see changes occurring. This is commonly used in ordering life histories, and the codes would be the stages in the life that appear to separate important segments, such as early life, first day of school, junior high, or becoming a teenager.

Activity Codes

Activity codes are directed at regularly occurring kinds of behaviors. These behaviors can be fairly obvious and relatively informal such as student smoking, joking, or school activities such as morning exercise in school, attendance, and lunch.

Event Codes

Event codes refer to happenings that occur infrequently or only once. Events such as the firing of a teacher, a teacher strike, and a school pageant are examples.

Strategy Codes

Strategies refer to the tactics, methods, and techniques people use to accomplish various things. Teachers' strategies to control students' behaviors, to teach reading, and to get out of recess duty are examples.

Relationship and Social Structure Codes

Regular patterns of behavior not officially defined by the organization such as cliques, friendships, romances, coalitions, enemies, or mentors fit under this category. Formal relations, such as social roles and positions, also belong here.

Methods Codes

The researcher's comments about the process, procedures, joys, and problems go here.

Working the data into codes is labor intensive and time consuming. Decide on what kind of piles, folders, or index cards you will use in advance. In an interview study with the homeless, Nihlen (1992) took all the interviews out and read them through several times:

> After reading 40 one-hour-long interviews fully transcribed you become desperate to reduce the work. The third time around I began to mark categories or codes which seemed to repeat from interview to interview. On index cards I recorded where these occurred in the text. For example, the category of "work" kept repeating itself. I made a code for "work," and put all the references each person made to work in this pile. I had many piles of cut up interviews on my desk and table after awhile and I began to think I needed to see what was in them.
>
> I took the pile coded "work" and sorted it into several more codes. Included in these piles were coding categories similar to the above such as setting/context, definition of the situation, perspectives held by participants, partici-

pants' ways of thinking about people and objects, process codes, etc. One coded pile which struck me I labeled "kinds of work." This could be an activity code. Under "kinds of work" I listed 8 jobs they talked about including canning (collecting cans), giving blood, signing (holding up a sign asking for work or money), and begging.

These codes and sub-codes helped me see that the homeless people I talked to were working, only at jobs that I had not considered as "real" jobs and therefore did not see until I was coding my data. These kinds of discoveries occur as you unpack your data in as many different ways as possible.

Discourse Analysis

Two primary types of discourse analysis exist in educational research. The first is based on grammatical theory and involves the study of discourse structures. The other concerns itself more with the discourse or text and uses it as evidence of larger social, political, cultural, and psychological processes. Gee, Michaels, and O'Connor (1992) present one of the most cogent and understandable discussions of this type of analysis. McKernan (1991) also discusses discourse analysis and presents the following categories.

Dilemma Analysis

In dilemma analysis, a researcher seeks out the dilemmas, tensions, or problems presented to the participants in the interviews. Perspective documents are organized so that each part of the dilemma analysis is presented for each of the participant roles interviewed. Each of these perspectives is checked with the participants. Thus, the individual's perspectives are mapped on the dilemma, resulting in perspectives from each participant in the scene (McKernan, 1991).

Constraints Analysis

Constraints analysis was developed for action researchers to determine the relative importance of teacher, school, and communal barriers to, or constraints on, doing action research. McKernan (1988) developed an instrument in connection with a study in which empirical evidence was collected from a variety of action research projects in the United States, Great Britain, and Ireland.

Content Analysis

Content analysis examines the linguistic deep meaning and structure of a message or communication. The message may be in a written communication or document, the media, or actual behavior. The goal is to uncover hidden themes and concepts in the message.

Content analyses of textbooks have demonstrated racist and sexist stereotyping by counting pictures of individuals and the type and frequency of minorities and white women in the photographs and analyzing the relative number of pages assigned to each group.

The procedure for doing content analysis includes the following:

1. Define the universe of the content—the text, message, or communication.
2. Write careful definitions of key categories being coded.
3. Analyze the data and code categories.
4. Quantify and do counts.

Document Analysis

Document analysis examines newspapers, minutes of meetings, articles, letters, diaries, and memos. These provide the researcher with facts pertaining to the subject and give insight into the organization, its history, and its purposes. Many practitioner researchers involve their students in the study of such primary sources of evidence.

Analysis of Personal Documents

The analysis of personal documents such as letters, diaries, poems, and autobiographies give insight into the author's mental life and are a revealing record.

Sociometric Analysis

A sociometric analysis measures emotional distance and determines a student's position within the classroom social structure. The researcher examines the choices made by each student in respect to the other students in the classroom. "Thus sociometry is invaluable for measuring and illuminating the complexities of classroom behavior and group dynamics—it is an ideal tool for classroom action research" (McKernan, 1991, p. 156). See Kerlinger (1986) and Hopkins (1985) for more information on how to do this type of analysis.

Episode Analysis

Episode analysis refers to the process of breaking down classroom discourse and events into small, codable units for analysis. The episodes need to have more than one participant, they need to be defined logically with boundaries of starting and ending, and they must be typical events that occur regularly in the environment.

Spradley's Ethnographic Analysis

Spradley (1979) developed three categories as tools for analyzing and ordering data: domain, taxonomic, and componential analyses. The method is based on semantic rules for aggregating differing units of data. Careful ethnographic, open-ended interviews and observations precede the analyses.

This is a lengthy and initially complicated process but many practitioners and university professors alike use portions of domain analysis to scan the data, then proceed with Spradley's or other analysis techniques. This type of analysis uses language to help us "see" what is happening and helps us build categories of meaning from data. Following is a brief description of the three categories.

Domain Analysis

A "domain" of cultural meaning is a category that includes smaller categories. For example, schools have students and teachers and other staff. "Kinds of teachers" could be a domain category. Each domain has terms, cover terms, and a semantic relationship that links

Included terms	Semantic relationship	Cover term
X	is a kind of	Y
Third-grade teachers	are a kind of	teacher
Resource room teachers	are a kind of	teacher
English as a second language teachers	are a kind of	teacher

Figure 5.9. Example of a Domain Analysis

together two categories. "Is a kind of" is a phrase that links two categories into a semantic relationship; its job is to place terms inside the cultural domain.

For example, using the cultural domain term "kinds of teachers," teachers can be identified as grade teachers (1st, 8th, 11th), special education teachers, or Chapter 1 reading teachers (see Figure 5.11). If you were doing a study in your school and during the interviews other teachers referred to the kinds of teachers mentioned above, you could place each term into the category "kind of teacher." Based on your interview and observational data, you would build numerous domain categories to help display and understand your data (see Figure 5.9).

Taxonomy

The next stage is to begin to ask questions that will help build a taxonomy; the researcher selects several cultural domains and makes sure that they include as many members as possible. Then the researcher seeks to find out how these domains are organized.

A taxonomy is a set of categories organized on the basis of a semantic relationship. It seeks to show the relationships among all the included terms in a domain. A taxonomy reveals subsets and how they are related to the whole. Using the above example of kinds of teachers, you could open the category of special education teachers to include C-level teachers, gifted teachers, resource room teachers, and full inclusion teachers.

Consider the school building. It is full of cultural meanings: which door the parents enter, and which doors staff more often enter; the

Library

Cafeteria

Classrooms
- Sixth grade
- Seventh grade
- Eighth grade

Principal's offices
- Front office
- Secretary's area
- Principal's room

Resource room

ESL room

Title V room

Teacher's lounge

Playground
- Baseball area
- Open field
- Metal gym equipment
- Hopscotch, jump rope area

Front of the school
- School bus area
- Visitor parking area
- Teachers' parking area

Figure 5.10. Example of a Taxonomy of the Term "School"

students' lunchroom, the library, the staff lounge, the principal's outer and inner office. Using a taxonomy of the term "school," one could build a diagram of the particular organization to understand it better (see Figure 5.10).

For strangers, this taxonomic analysis would help them orient themselves in the building. For a researcher who knows the school intimately, it might help to make the familiar strange to remember all the areas in which students are not allowed, or only allowed during certain scheduled periods. For example, if you found two seventh graders hanging around out in front of the building an hour before school ended, you might come to certain conclusions about the appropriateness of their behavior and activity.

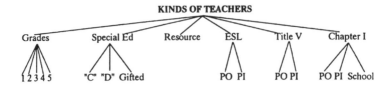

Figure 5.11. Example of a Taxonomy of Kinds of Teachers

Another way to build a taxonomy is shown in Figure 5.11, using the domain "kinds of teachers."

Componential Analysis

The third category used by Spradley is the componential analysis, which is a systematic search for the units of meaning associated with the cultural patterns of people. When contrasts exist among members of a domain, those contrasts are attributes or components of meaning. Component is another term for unit; thus, a researcher is looking for the units of meaning that people have assigned to their cultural categories.

Returning to the example of teachers as a domain category, what you seek to discover at this stage are the actual components of meaning the participants use when discussing kinds of teachers. Spradley suggests seeking out through interviews, observations, and your own notes the dimensions of contrast in, for example, identifying one kind of teacher from another. Location, training, tools of the trade, and status of subject taught would all be components of meaning, attributes associated with the cultural category of resource room teacher.

Analytic Induction

In the most general sense, analytic induction helps build units of compiled data into constructs that hold true and do not damage the truth of the data.

Loose hypotheses and typologies are tested against the data; negative cases are sought to expand, adapt, or restrict initial existing codes. These constructs are then loosely coupled with various theoretical frameworks as the researcher seeks to find a match that will do justice to the data and the theory. Theory, in this case, can and often does provide a useful framework that can help generalize data so that other people can better understand the research site and its meaning.

LeCompte and Preissle (1993) are a good resource to read about this type of analysis, as are Lincoln and Guba (1985) on a similar analysis mode, negative case analysis.

Mehan (1979) writes about a multiethnic school and uses analytic induction to analyze classroom interaction data. He calls his method "constitutive ethnography."

Constant Comparison

The constant comparison method of analysis comes from the work of Glaser and Strauss (1967); as soon as a researcher begins to collect data, he or she also begins coding it and examining it in the light of more data. Thus, the researcher is constantly collecting, coding, analyzing, and comparing data. Analysis generation also proceeds along this path. As newly collected data on events are compared with earlier notes, new typologies and relationships become apparent. See LeCompte and Preissle (1993) for a summary and Glaser and Strauss (1967) for a detailed description of this method.

Standardized Observational Protocols

Standardized observational protocols refer to research tools such as checklists and rating scales discussed in the observation section. In this format, the researcher has already determined what he or she will look at, and has built predetermined observational categories and weighted them appropriately. The researcher analyzes the results and codes the field data into the predetermined categories. On the one hand, this is considered the least qualitative mode of analysis because it does not assume that the cultural scene studied will generate the codes, or that others can be added. However, for practitioner researchers who are daily in their school or classroom, this can be an important data-gathering tool due to its static nature and ease of completion. Given the subjective and emic nature of the practitioner researcher's relationship to the site, standardized observational protocols are often useful and informative tools. See Amidon and Flanders (1963) and Mehan (1979) for further information on this technique.

Multiple Methods Studies

This section is included to give practitioner researchers an opportunity to consider the combination of various techniques into a holistic study such as an ethnography, oral history, or case study. Because of the breadth and comprehensiveness of such studies, long-term, collaborative research is almost a given.

In its most fundamental form, almost any technique in qualitative or quantitative research can be combined with other techniquess to enrich a study. Triangulation can help keep a practitioner researcher clear on the difference between his or her views and the views of other participants in the study. It also gives a researcher other perspectives from which to view the data. Following are examples of several kinds of possible combinations.

Educational Ethnography

An educational ethnography is a holistic view of an entire cultural scene such as a school and its community or a classroom. It focuses on the culture of the scene, for example, the cultural transmission occurring, and the total and comprehensive view of this scene. For example, in a study of a classroom, you would include information on the room and its context and placement within the school and community. You would also include language, teachers and aides, support staff, the coming and going of adults and children, complete demographic information on every person in the room, physical composition of the room, maps of floor plans and walls, and the temporal schedule. You would be focussing on various aspects of the classroom and would include complete information on these aspects.

If you were looking at the multicultural curriculum in a classroom, you might interview the teacher and aide and support staff, as well as the principal, Title V and VII workers, district staff, and community members. You could also do a content analysis of material culture in the room: reading and trade books, workbooks, pictures, and wall hangings. You might want to dig into the archives and do some historical reconstruction at the district and state levels, looking at state and local legislation, district and state policy statements, and federal guidelines to understand how this classroom came to be a multicultural space. You could gather the test scores of the children over a period of years to compare how the new curriculum has enhanced their learning.

Lastly, you could do observations of the classroom and record which children played and interacted regularly with which children, and how the teacher interacted with each child. You could also observe how each child reacted to the multicultural curriculum, and how the teacher taught. You could do the same kind of observations with support staff and the principal. The more comprehensive you are, the better the study will be and the more information you will obtain. Using different methods enhances the variety of data you gather and makes it possible to make the familiar strange.

All this takes years to complete, and you would likely be working collaboratively with others to collect data. The action research spiral of planning, acting, observing, reflecting, and revising is crucial to such an undertaking.

Excellent examples of ethnographies of schooling have been done primarily by academics to date. See Fine (1991), Jackson (1968), Lubek (1985), McLaren (1989), McNeil (1986), Ogbu (1974), Smith and Geoffrey (1968), and Wolcott (1973).

Oral History

Oral histories rely primarily on open-ended, ethnographic, multiple interviews with a series of persons involved in a particular cultural scene or issue. Often archival research is involved in building a well-rounded picture of the lives and times of the people interviewed. For example, if you are interviewing older teachers on how they worked in multicultural classrooms in the 1940s and 1950s, you might want to read the local newspapers to find out how the community approached this issue, if it did at all. You also might read educational journals about earlier theories of multiculturalism. And, as with most archival studies of education, the local school board and state board of education provide invaluable information on trends and directives to teachers.

Case Studies

A case study is narrowly focused on a particular person, site, or scene. It is an instance drawn from a class. "By concentrating on a single phenomenon or entity (the case), this approach aims to uncover the interaction of significant factors characteristic of the phenomenon." (Merriam, 1991, p. 10). Case studies do not draw from any specific methodology or theory; however, interviewing is the primary technique. They also include investigation of archival records, testing scores, and personal documents. The case study seeks to create an idealized type of person, event, or site and to show how the case represents this ideal even as it is individualized.

See Janesick (1982) for her study of classroom group processes through a case study. See Merriam (1991) on how to conduct a case study, and Yin (1989).

6

Toward a New Paradigm

Practitioner researchers are greatly interested in naturalistic research methods. Martin (1987), likening schools and classrooms to communities, makes an impassioned call to teachers to become the ethnographers of schools and classrooms:

> Ethnographic research in education sets out to describe not only events in classrooms which occur as students and teachers work, speak, write, interrupt, question, etc., but also describe all that can be observed and reported about the contexts of lessons, that is, events in the school and in the students' home lives that bear on what goes on in the classroom. . . . The chief characteristic of this kind of data is that the documentation (description and records) is made by people who were present at the time, and who can, therefore, describe experience as it was lived. First hand accounts differ in important ways from reports by people who were not there, or were not part of the community. (p. 20)

This call to draw on the naturalistic paradigm, of which ethnography is a part, emphasizes both the holistic nature of this type of research and the advantages of its being done by "insiders" who are immersed in the reality being described.

Practitioner researchers everywhere are taking up Martin's challenge to do ethnographies of schools and classrooms from the inside. However, many are stumbling on problems that their university research classes have not prepared them to solve. We have already discussed the political problems, but another set of methodological problems must be dealt with—the adaptation of traditional qualitative methods to become usable in the real world of schools by already overburdened practitioners.

Pearson (1993), the teacher from Chapter 5 who was attempting to begin a classroom study of "discipline," said, "As I began my observations, I realized that I had not yet learned the 'tricks of the trade '" (p. 6). She describes her harried day and how she was unable to take notes in class while she taught; nor could she find the time to do sociograms or transcribe videotaped classroom data. She ended up blaming herself by internalizing her "failure" and concluded that trying "to solve this problem has given me a new insight into myself. I always thought of myself as organized. . . . I think there are levels of being organized, something like the levels of thinking skills. I'm still at the factual level. I'm obsessed with doing it, but haven't the understanding of it yet" (p. 6).

This tendency to blame oneself for not "measuring up" or for not learning the "tricks of the trade" is all too common among practitioner researchers. Part of the problem may be that practitioner researchers are learning tricks for the wrong trade. Academic qualitative researchers do not have to juggle data gathering with teaching or administering a school. The methods presented in Chapter 5, although potentially useful, were not designed with practitioners in mind.

A theme of this book is the gap between the call for teachers to be researchers in their schools and classrooms and the lack of discussion about how one manages to perform two full-time jobs simultaneously: that of being an educational practitioner and that of being an educational researcher.

This situation seems like a lose-lose situation for practitioners. To do the work as thoroughly as outsider research demands, they must sacrifice time with students (not to mention their evenings and weekends); and yet if they do not do research like academic researchers, their work is labeled second class by the criteria of the naturalistic paradigm. Practitioners doing site-based dissertations may be willing to sacrifice for a year or two, but what about the practitioner who wants to do research as part of being a professional educator or to improve his or her own practice?

Few practitioners working in school settings currently get release time for research. Although this is a fairly standard "perk" in academe, it is virtually unheard of in most elementary and secondary school settings. Writing, publishing, and gaining tenure reward a university scholar's desire to do research; many practitioner researchers labor to do research despite the fact that it is not a part of their job description, a description already full of challenging demands on time and energy.

The issue is even more serious than that of a lack of fit between traditional qualitative methods and practitioner realities. Using the methodological tenets of the naturalistic paradigm to guide practitioner researchers is a deficit model in which school practitioners come off as "disadvantaged" or even inept. "Anthropology was built on the notion of the primitive and the outsider, of practice and the theorizer, and of the researched and the researcher. This is the very kind of mental/manual divide which the proponents of teacher research wish to overcome" (Lawn, 1989, p. 159). Qualitative field methods can add to the practitioner researcher's repertoire of methods, but practitioners need to appropriate them carefully.

Two questions are related to this discussion: What do practitioners gain in adding a research component to their roles as educators that helps offset the demands in time and energy? How can qualitative methods be appropriated and adapted to "work" in the real world of practitioners and schools? In other words: Why do practitioner research?

For the past few years, Herr has worked with a middle school teacher to improve her practice. At one point, the teacher's chairperson, the teacher, and Herr sat in the teacher's classroom, reviewing her latest round of student evaluations; the results were devastating, and all three struggled to understand the negative feedback from the students. The teacher was a ready learner, eager for and quick to try suggestions that others offered. The hoped-for results still seemed out of reach.

The chairperson, a supportive ally in working with his department member, was visibly discouraged and worried. The teacher became teary and wondered whether she had what it took to succeed in this profession. Herr suggested that this teacher might be a good candidate to do some practitioner research; the opportunity for the teacher to observe her own classroom in some systematic way might help her reflect and gain insight into her own practice. The chairperson, worrying about adding the burden of research to an already over-burdened and discouraged teacher, wondered out loud if this might not be "too much" in addition to daily classroom preparations and other school obligations. The teacher replied that what was "too much" was the constant drain of living with unsolved practice problems; the thought of a systematic inquiry that might shed light on class-room problems felt like a lifeline, to which she eagerly grabbed hold.

There is no miracle end to the story; now the teacher is embark-ing on her own inquiry of her classroom with the support of her chairperson and with consultation from Herr. The hope is that her self-discovery process will help unravel the mysteries of her teach-ing and improve her practice.

Accounts like Richards' (1989) speak to the potential benefits of practitioner research. The possibility of some insight and positive problem solving where "hopeless" practice issues are concerned can be a solid motivator for beginning some form of practitioner research.

The opposite can be true as well: Excited that through the trial and error of refining our own practices we may have hit upon something that really works, the thought of systematizing informal observations of our practice and then disseminating the results to a wider audience can be an attractive option. An example of this comes from Herr's experience in the school in which she works as a counselor.

> I remember a conversation I had with a math teacher regard-ing a student I was concerned about; although academically able, the student was doing miserably in every class—ex-cept for math. I had approached the math teacher, hoping she could give me some insight into what "works" with this

student. As we talked together, the teacher recounted that she had been doing some experimenting with her classroom set up, weaving more cooperative learning experiences into her math classes. She had noticed that her female students in particular seemed to enjoy the times the class worked in cooperative groupings; grades of the girls previously struggling seemed to be on their way up and the teacher felt convinced that cooperative learning had something to do with it. As someone acquainted with the research literature showing that middle school is a particularly trying time for female adolescents, that self-esteem plummets and grades, particularly in math and science, drop, I can remember feeling exhilarated by this teacher's observations. I would be excited for her to consider doing some practitioner research as a means to systematically record and test her hunch regarding what was happening in her classroom. (Herr, 1993)

We need this teacher's findings as well as those of other practitioners as we work to understand how to create better learning environments for middle school students, particularly girls.

The importance of investigating and recording what works is particularly important in light of the difficult problems facing educators and the public discourse highlighting what does not work in our schools. As insiders in the system, practitioners have a unique vantage point from which to problem solve. For example, in the study done by Ballenger (1993), it was only because of her unique status as an insider that she was able to make meaning of the students' relationships and connect her observations to a challenge of existing theories.

Many are becoming convinced that practitioners have a lot to gain through systematic observation and intervention in our own practice sites; in addition, there is a growing sense that practitioner researchers can help inform the larger knowledge base of education through our findings. The challenge is to create ways to do the research without overwhelming ourselves in the process; to make research an integral part of what we already do, rather than merely an "add-on."

Methodological Adaptations: Practitioners Looking for Appropriate Techniques

The last thing educators need is one more thing to do. How can current functions in an educator's day be integrated into the role of researcher? What does the day-to-day operation of a classroom or school site offer in the way of data? Educators are answering this question in many ways. Many teachers are finding that they can use student assignments in ways that lend themselves to data collection. Dicker (1990) used student journals to give her the student perspective on things she was attempting in the classroom; she would have had them keeping journals anyway—but in focusing their journals on topics that she wanted information about, she combined two goals: having her students write and data collection:

> Students wrote journals during the last 10 minutes of each class or for homework. Not only did this deepen the students' thinking about their work, but it provided me with a different perspective on the events that were happening in the class. Anticipating that students might need some assistance in writing the journal, I posed several questions for them to answer. (p. 204)

In a footnote at the end of her article, Dicker (1990) gives examples of the questions she posed for journal writing: "What do you feel you have learned so far in this course? Which activities have you enjoyed the most and why?" (p. 209). She continues her reflections on the integration of an assignment with its use as a source of data:

> The students' journal writing was not only educationally valid as an assignment that encouraged writing skills as they reflected on their experiences in the class and organized their thoughts, but it also provided a basis for my future planning. The knowledge gained from my reading and reflection on the student journals became an integral part of my own journal as I commented on student writings. (p. 204)

Dicker was already using her own journal as a source of data, so the writings of students offered her their perspectives on the same classroom experiences that she herself was writing about.

Richards (1989), in asking herself how to motivate the "bums" of 8H, found herself reading the research literature on motivation to gather ideas both for her teaching and her research. She designed a 2-week teaching unit on motivation based on her reading; Richards gave the students the benefit of the information she was reading and found a direct use for it in her classroom. She got feedback on motivating factors from her students in the form of a writing assignment.

Many teachers fear that their research efforts, while potentially improving practice, will take time away from their real function: Spending time with students in educationally meaningful ways. Some educators are integrating their students directly into their research effort as coinvestigators. Richards (1989) read her research proposal to her students and included them in the process of working to discover motivating factors in the classroom. They directly discussed in the classroom issues that the research was raising.

For Herr, as a school counselor, interviewing for her research efforts often gives her access to students she would not necessarily see as a counselor; the research interview can be a nonthreatening way for students previously unknown to her to get to know her. The fact that she is seeking them out for research purposes allows them to link with her without the stigma of identifying themselves as in need of counseling. In her experience, it is not unusual that these interviewees, having now been inside the counselor's door once, return on their own.

Herr also notes that the research interview can be seen as part of a therapeutic intervention, raising with students issues that they may or may not have reflected on before, but that, once encountered, offer material for further thought. For example, in her current research on adolescent sexual decision making, Herr is finding that as students respond to questions regarding the decisions they make, and they present a wealth of information that they may choose to work on therapeutically at another time.

One last thought is in order. There is no doubt that embarking on practitioner research reorders an educator's priorities. For example, a teacher may choose to spend time with students in ways that directly impact her research while opting out of other activities in the school. Herr, for example, chose to chaperon student dances and took a sociologist's view in watching the evenings' events. She later wrote in her journal about her observations of student romances on the dance floor and linked these observations to her study of students' sexual decision making; chaperoning a school basketball game may not have afforded her the same opportunity.

A data source often overlooked by academic researchers is the artifacts that the students themselves produce, as well as the documents that the school produces. These represent "ready-made" data; many practitioners incorporate them into their studies. Although most of these studies involve the examination of student writing samples, many also analyze student drawings (for an example, see Awbrey, 1989) or material culture as discussed on p. 147.

Methods That Surface Tacit Knowledge

One way to address the danger of practitioner research not "measuring up" to the standards of traditional qualitative research is to emphasize the ways that practitioner research is more rigorous than qualitative research. Practitioner researchers can take a lesson from qualitative researchers, who for decades were viewed as less rigorous than their quantitative counterparts. Qualitative researchers did not try to measure up to the positivists' criteria of rigor, but rather emphasized their own claims to rigorous research.

If the goal of educational research is to produce knowledge about educational practice that will bring about improvements in practice, who knows educational practice better than those who act daily in school settings? Naturalistic researchers know that the knowledge they write up in field notes is only a fraction of the knowledge they possess. They are also aware that as they analyze their field data, their tacit knowledge of the setting is continually brought into play. Although school practitioners may not be able to take field notes with the care and regularity of a naturalistic researcher, their tacit knowledge of the setting runs much deeper than that of the outside observer. This is not only because they spend more time in the setting, but also because they must continually interact with it.

This helps explain why keeping a journal is a marginal research technique for naturalistic researchers and a primary one for practitioners. Naturalistic researchers tend to use journals as a supplement to field notes in which they monitor their own personal biases. For practitioners, the journal, in a sense, acts as their field notes. This does not mean that practitioners should not continue to find systematic ways to record the flow of classroom or school behavior, but rather that practitioners surface their tacit knowledge about their settings through journals.

Chapter 3 offers rich examples of the journal writing process as educators are currently using it in their research. In our review of practitioner research, writing journals was one of the most common research techniques being used. Journals offer an effective way to bring to a conscious level all that the practitioners have observed and absorbed in the course of a day's work; they also represent a generative process—writing daily journals forces practitioners to systematize their thoughts and record them in a fashion that readies them for another round of work built on the previous day's base.

Dicker (1990) writes about the function her journal served in her research:

> Following the recommendations of Kemmis and McTaggart (1982), the major data collection device was my own reflective journal or diary, written each evening following a class period. The journal had two purposes: to shed a focused light on the previous lesson and to clarify plans for the following lesson. It was in fact a record of my thinking, revealing my practical knowledge and the particular way it was held and used. A further reflection was written each weekend in order to extend and deepen the reflections on the week's work and to develop a sufficiently thick description for the study. (p. 204)

In facing the time constraints that are part of their lives, some practitioners have experimented with tape recording their thoughts, that is, oral journals, sometimes while driving home from their school settings. Others tape record their class sessions or research settings and listen to them on the way home or later in the day to help them recall events of the day; then they write in their journals when they have the opportunity. Dicker (1990) writes, "Not only did the tapes capture the 'teacher-in-action' but, like the student journals, they also provided a student perspective. The tape recordings were a valuable check on the accuracy of my interpretations as I analyzed my journal" (p. 204).

Anderson and Herr have experimented with tape recording their debriefing sessions at the end of the school day, sharing stories of the day while analyzing them; they capture on tape the story telling as well as the ideas germinating from the dialogues.

Although practitioner research has tended to use the naturalistic research paradigm as a basis for creating an alternative paradigm, a paradigm already exists that better lends itself to the practitioner's purposes—Schon's (1993) elaboration of "reflection in action." Altrichter and Posch (1989) ask, "What should a methodological model which could serve as an orientation for teacher research look like?" (p. 29). After reviewing Schon's model and comparing it to extant social science models, Altrichter and Posch conclude that

> it is not necessary for teacher research to rely on imported methodological criteria from other fields of research, but it should concentrate on further developing reflective features of professional action which in the context of practice itself are responsible for enhancing the quality of action, such as defining problems by naming and framing, combining advocacy with inquiry, and feeding back a more holistic appreciation of action results to the original problem definition. (Altrichter and Posch, 1989, pp. 29-30)

Cochran-Smith and Lytle (1993) elaborate on the potential of a humanities-oriented approach to practitioner research. Our purpose here is not to discuss the pros and cons of the humanities or Schon's model, but rather to suggest that practitioner research may be well served by exploring alternatives to social science paradigms, which fail to appreciate the strengths of the tacit and narrative ways of knowing that are so important to practitioners (see also Longstreet, 1982).

Working in a Community of Inquiry: Buffering the Isolation

In reviewing accounts of practitioner research, one finds examples of practitioners doing research with others in their schools or consciously joining a research group. Chapter 3 discusses several examples of the involvement of groups in the research process: the principals' group (Christman et al., in press) was formed to gain the insight of other administrators as well as to support each of them in the work and research processes. The Educators' Forum (Evans, 1989; Stubbs, 1989) was specifically formed to generate practitioner research. Russell (1992) moved to involve others when she formed dialogue groups for teachers.

Part of the appeal of working with others in the research process reflects a practical view: We gain other bodies to help with the work, whether it is reflecting on methods and data with us, or helping with data gathering. Teachers with student teachers have utilized their presence to help observe or free themselves to gather data during the school day; some teachers and student teachers have experimented with engaging in a joint research project, both contributing to the data gathering and collecting (Anderson et al., 1992). Other colleagues have "traded" observation time, going in and out of each others' classrooms during their free periods; each gains another set of eyes on the research processes. Practitioners living in areas with a local university can sometimes enlist the help of graduate students who may be assigned the exercise of observing school settings.

Dicker (1990) discusses her use of a colleague as a "critical friend." She enlisted the help of a former English teacher to read her journal; the teacher asked questions based on what she was reading, pushing Dicker to further thought and explanation of what she was doing and observing.

Conclusion

We have only scratched the surface of the dilemmas that practitioner researchers are struggling with. Building a new paradigm is hard work, and it must remain tentative lest criteria congeal too soon. Ultimately, practitioners must determine the criteria.

If there is a common thread in comments that practitioner researchers make, it is the discovery of becoming a learner again. Rosenholtz (1989) found that most teachers reported that it took 3 years to learn to be a teacher. According to most teachers, after 3 years they pretty much "had it down" and could consider themselves no longer a learner. In contrast practitioner research is above all else a project of lifelong learning. Duckworth (1986) discusses how teaching and research flow naturally back and forth during a teacher's day. She describes how the vocation of teaching requires a researching, learning spirit. We give her the last word:

> This kind of researcher would be a teacher in the sense of caring about some part of the world and how it works enough to want to make it accessible to others; she would be fascinated by the questions of how to engage people in it and how people make sense of it; she would have time and resources to pursue these questions to the depth of her interest, to write what she learned, and to contribute to theoretical and pedagogical discussions on the nature and development of human learning.
>
> And then I wonder—why should this be a separate research profession? There is no reason I can think of not to rearrange the resources available for education so that this description defines the job of the public school teacher.
>
> So this paper ends with a romance. But then, it began with a passion. (p. 495)

References

Altricher, H., & Posch, P. (1989). Does the grounded theory approach offer a guiding paradigm for teacher research? *Cambridge Journal of Education, 19*(1), 21-40.

Amidon, E. J., & Flanders, N. A. (1963). *The role of the teacher in the classroom: A manual for understanding and improving teachers' classroom behavior.* Minneapolis: Amidon.

Anderson, C., Butts, J., Lett, P., Mansdoerfer, S., & Raisch, M. (1992). *Las ventanas abiertas/open windows: Teachers researching the teaching of writing.* Unpublished manuscript.

Anderson, G. L. (1990). Toward a critical constructivist approach to school administration: Invisibility, legitimation, and the study of non-events. *Educational Administration Quarterly, 26*(1), 38-59.

Anderson, G. L. (1991). Cognitive politics of principals and teachers: Ideological control in an elementary school. In J. Blase (Ed.), *The politics of life in schools: Power, conflict and cooperation* (pp. 120-138). Newbury Park: Sage.

Anderson, G. L., & Herr, K. (1993). The micro-politics of student voices: Moving from diversity of bodies to diversity of voices in schools. In C. Marshall (Ed.), *The new politics of race and gender* (pp. 58-68). Washington, DC: Falmer Press.

Argyris, C., Putnam, R., & Smith, D. M. (1985). *Action science: Concepts, methods, and skills for research and intervention.* San Francisco: Jossey-Bass.

Argyris, C., & Schon, D. (1974). *Theory in practice: Increasing professional effectiveness.* San Francisco: Jossey-Bass.

Argyris, C., & Schon, D. (1991). Participatory action research and action science compared: A commentary. In W. F. Whyte (Ed.), *Participatory action research* (pp. 85-96). Newbury Park, CA: Sage.

Atwell, N. (1982). Classroom-based writing research: Teachers learn from students. *English Journal, 71,* 84-87.

Awbrey, M. (1989). A teacher's action research study of writing in the kindergarten: Accepting the natural expression of children. *Peabody Journal of Education, 64*(2), 33-64.

Bailey, J., Brazee, J., Chiavaroli, S., Herbeck, J., Lechner, T., Lewis, D., McKittrick, A., Reid, K., Robinson, B., & Spear, H. (1988). Problem solving our way to alternative evaluation procedures. *Language Arts, 65*(4), 364-373.

Ballenger, C. (1993). Learning the ABC's: The shadow curriculum. In *Children's voices, teachers' stories: Papers from the Brookline Teacher Researcher Seminar.* Technical Report N. 11. Newton, MA: Literacies Institute.

Bateson, G., & Mead, M. (Producers and directors). (1942). *Balinese character: A photographic analysis* [Film]. New York: New York Academy of Science.

Belanger, J. (1992). Teacher research as a lifelong experiment. *English Journal, 81*(8), 16-23.

Berger, P., & Luckmann, T. (1967). *The social construction of reality.* Garden City, NJ: Anchor.

Berlak, A., & Berlak, H. (1981). *Dilemmas of schooling: Teaching and social change.* London: Methuen.

Bicklen, S. (1973). *Lessons of consequence: Women's perceptions of their elementary school experience: A retrospective study.* Unpublished doctoral dissertation, University of Massachusetts.

Bissex, G., & Bullock, R. (1987). *Seeing for ourselves: Case study research by teachers of writing.* Portsmouth, NH: Heinemann.

Blanchard, K., & Johnson, S. (1982). *The one minute manager.* New York: Berkeley Publishing Group.

Bogdan, R., & Biklen, S. K. (1982). *Qualitative research for education: An introduction to theory and methods.* Boston: Allyn & Bacon.

Brady, J. (1979). *The craft of interviewing.* New York: Vintage.

Bragstad, L. B., & Stumpf, S. T. (1982). *A guidebook for teaching study skills and motivation.* Boston: Allyn & Bacon.

Brause, R. S., & Mayher, J. S. (1991). *Search and re-search: What the inquiring teacher needs to know.* New York: Falmer Press.

Brown, L. D., & Tandon, R. (1983). Ideology and political inquiry: Action research and participatory research. *The Journal of Applied Behavioral Science, 19*(3), 277-294.

Brown, L. M., & Gilligan, C. (1992). *Meeting at the crossroads: Women's psychology and girl's development.* Cambridge, MA: Harvard University Press.

Broyles, I. (1991, February). *Transforming teacher leadership through action research.* Paper presented at the annual meeting of the New England Educational Research Association, Portsmouth, NH.

Bruner, J. (1986). *Actual minds, possible worlds.* Cambridge, MA: Harvard University Press.

Calhoun, E. F. (1993). Action research: Three approaches. *Educational Leadership, 51*(2), 62-65.

Calhoun, E. F., & Glickman, C. D. (1993, April). *Issues and dilemmas of action research in the League of Professional Schools.* Paper presented at the annual meeting of the American Educational Research Association, Atlanta.

Carr, W. (1989). Action research: Ten years on. *Journal of Curriculum Studies, 21,* 85-90.

Carr, W., & Kemmis, S. (1983). *Becoming critical: Knowing through action research.* Victoria, BC: Deakin University Press.

Cazden, C., Diamondstone, J., & Naso, P. (1988, April). *Relationships between teacher research and researcher research on writing instruction.* Paper presented at the annual meeting of the American Educational Research Association, New Orleans.

Chisholm, L. (1990). Action research: Some methodological and political considerations. *British Educational Research Journal, 16*(3), 249-257.

Chism, N., Sanders, D., & Zitlow, C. (1989). Observations on a faculty development program based on practice-centered inquiry. *Peabody Journal of Education, 64*(3), 1-23.

Christman, J., Hirshman, J., Holtz, A., Perry, H., Spelkoman, R., & Williams, M. (in press). Doing Eve's work: Women principals write about their practice. *Anthropology and Education Quarterly.*

Cobb, K. (1993). *Meaningful learning experiences: Perceptions of middle school students.* Unpublished manuscript.

Cochran-Smith, M., & Lytle, S. (1993). *Inside/outside: Teacher research and knowledge.* New York: Teachers College Press.

Coles, R. (1989). *The call of stories: Teaching and the moral imagination.* Boston: Houghton Mifflin.

Collier, Jr., J. (1967). *Visual anthropology : Photography as a research method.* New York: Holt, Rinehart & Winston.

Connelly, F. M., & Clandinin, J. (1987). On narrative method, biography and narrative unities in the study of teaching. *Journal of Educational Thought, 21*(3), 332-456.

Connelly, F. M., & Clandinin, J. (1988). *Teachers as curriculum planners: Narratives of experience.* New York: Teachers College Press.

Connelly, F. M., & Clandinin, J. (1990). Stories of experience and narrative inquiry. *Educational Researcher, 19*(5), 2-14.

Corey, S. M. (1949). Action research, fundamental research, and educational practices. *Teachers College Record, 50,* 509-514.

Corey, S. M. (1953). *Action research to improve school practices.* New York: Teachers College Press.

Corey, S. M. (1954). Action research in education. *Journal of Educational Research, 47,* 375-380.

Counts, G. (1932). *Dare the school build a new social order?* New York: John Day Co.

Crawford, M., & Marecek, J. (1989). Feminist theory, feminist psychology: A bibliography of epistemology, critical analysis and applications. *Psychology of Women Quarterly, 13,* 477-491.

Cunningham, J. B. (1983). Gathering data in a changing organization. *Human relations, 36*(5), 403-420.

Delpit, L. (1986). Skills and other dilemmas of a progressive black educator. *Harvard Educational Review, 56*(4), 379-385.

Denzin, N., & Lincoln, Y. (1994). *The handbook of qualitative research.* Thousand Oaks, CA: Sage.

de Schutter, A., & Yopo, B. (1981). *Investigación participativa: Una opción metodológica para la educatión de adultos.* Pátzcuaro, Michoacan, México: CREFAL.

Dewey, J. (1916). *Democracy and education.* New York: Macmillan.

Dicker, M. (1990). Using action research to navigate an unfamiliar teaching assignment. *Theory into Practice, 29*(3), 203-208.

Diegmueller, K. (1992, August). Dynamic duo. *Teacher Magazine,* 23-27.

Duckworth, E. (1986). Teaching as research. *Harvard Educational Review, 56*(4), 481-495.

Dunaway, D., & Baum, W. (1984). *Oral history: An interdisciplinary anthology.* Nashville: Oral History Association.

Elliot, J. (1991). *Action research for educational change.* Philadelphia: Open University Press.

Ellwood, C. M. (1993). Can we really look through our students' eyes? An urban teacher's perspective. *Educational Foundations, 7*(3), 63-78.

Erickson, F. (1973). What makes school ethnography "ethnographic?" *CAE Newsletter, 4*(2), 10-19.

Erickson, F. (1986). *Tasks in times: Objects of study in a natural history of teaching.* East Lansing: Institute for Research on Teaching, Michigan State University.

Evans, C. (1989, April). *The educators' forum: Teacher-initiated research in progress.* Paper presented at the annual meeting of the American Educational Research Association, San Francisco.

Evans, C., Stubbs, M., Duckworth, E., & Davis, C. (1981). *Teacher-initiated research: Professional development for teachers and a method for defining research based on practice.* Cambridge, MA: Technical Education Research Centers.

Evans, C., Stubbs, M., Frechette, P. Neely, C., & Warner, J. (1987). *Educational practitioners: Absent voices in the building of educational theory.* Wellesley, MA: Wellesley College Center for Research on Women.

Fals Borda, O. (1979). Investigating reality in order to transform it. *Dialectical Anthropology, 4*(1), 33-56.

Faust, M. A. (1993). "It's not a perfect world": Defining success and failure at Central Park East Secondary School. In R. Donmoyer & R, Kos (Eds.), *At-risk students: Portraits, policies, programs, and practices* (pp. 323-342). Albany: State University of New York Press.

Feldman, A. (1992, February). *Institutionalized action research and teachers' lives: The role of the facilitator in the California "100 schools" project.* Paper presented at the Annual Ethnography in Education Research Forum, Philadelphia.

Fernandes, W., & Tandon, R. (1981). *Participatory research and evaluation: Experiments in research as a process of liberation.* New Delhi: Indian Social Institute.

Fine, M. (1991). *Framing dropouts: Notes on the politics of an urban public high school.* Albany: State University of New York Press.

Foshay, A. W. (1993, April). *Action research: An early history in the U.S.* Paper presented at the annual meeting of the American Educational Research Association, Atlanta.

Foshay, A. W., & Wann, K. (1953). *Children's social values: An action research study.* New York: Bureau of Publications, Teachers College.

Foucault, M. (1980). *Power/knowledge: Selected interviews and other writings, 1972-1977.* New York: Pantheon.

Frank, A. (1952). *The diary of a young girl.* New York: Doubleday.

Freedman, S., Jackson, J., & Boles, K. (1983). Teaching: An imperiled profession. In L. Shulman & G. Sykes (Eds.), *Handbook of teaching and policy* (pp. 261-299). New York: Longman.

Freedman, S., Jackson, J., & Boles, K. (1986). *The effect of teaching on teachers.* Grand Forks: University of North Dakota Press.

Freire, P. (1970). *Pedagogy of the oppressed.* New York: Herder & Herder.

Frechette, P. (1987). Learning to observe Joshua. *Pathways, 4*(1), 7-17.

Fullan, M. (1982). *The meaning of educational change.* New York: Teachers College Press.

Fulwiler, T. (1987). *The journal book.* Portsmouth, NH: Boynton/ Cook.

Garcia, G. (1991). *Learning and culture: Teachers as agents of change in professional development schools.* Unpublished manuscript.

Gaventa, J. (1988). Participatory research in North America: A perspective on participatory research in Latin America. *Convergence: An International Journal of Adult Education. 21*(2-3), 19-48.

Gaventa, J., & Horton, B. D. (1981). A citizen's research project in Appalachia, USA. *Convergence: An International Journal of Adult Education, 14*(3), 30-42.

Gearing, F., & Sangree, L. (1979). *Toward a cultural theory of education and schooling*. New York: Mouton Press.

Gee, J. P., Michaels, S., & O'Connor, M. C. (1992). Discourse analysis. In M. D. LeCompte, W. L. Millroy, & J. Preissle (Eds.), *The handbook of qualitative research in education* (pp. 227-291). San Diego: Academic Press.

Geertz, C. (1973). *The interpretation of cultures*. New York: Basic Books.

Gitlin, A., Bringhurst, K., Burns, M., Cooley, V., Myers, B. Price, K., Russell, R., & Tiess, P. (1992). *Teachers' voices for school change*. New York: Teachers College Press.

Glaser, B. G., & Strauss, A. L. (1967). *The discovery of grounded theory: Strategies for qualitative research*. Chicago: Aldine.

Glickman, C. D., & Allen, L. (1991). *Lessons from the field: Renewing schools through shared governance and action research*. Athens: Program for School Improvement, University of Georgia.

Gluck, S., & Patai, D. (1991). *Women's words: The feminist practice of oral history*. New York: Routledge.

Gore, J., & Zeichner, K. (1991). Action research and reflective teaching in preservice teacher education: A case study from the United States. *Teaching and Teacher Education, 7*(2), 119-136.

Goswami, D., & Schultz, J. (1993). *Reclaiming the classroom: Teachers and students together*. Portsmouth, NH: Boynton/Cook.

Goswami, D., & Stillman, P. R. (1987). *Reclaiming the classroom: Teacher research as an agency for change*. Upper Montclair, NJ: Boynton.

Graves, D. (1981a). Research update: Where have all the teachers gone? *Language Arts, 58*(1), 492-497.

Graves, D. (1981b). Research update: A new look at writing research. *Language Arts, 58*(2), 197-206.

Green, J., & Chandler, S. (1990). Toward a dialogue about implementation within a conceptual cycle of inquiry. In E. Guba (Ed.), *The paradigm dialogue* (pp. 202-224). Newbury Park: Sage.

Greene, J. (1992). The practitioner's perspective. *Curriculum Inquiry, 22*, 39-45.

Griffin, E., Lieberman, A., & Jacullo-Noto, J. (1982). *Interactive research and development of schooling*. Final Report. New York: Teachers College Press.

Gutièrrez, L. M. (1990). Working with women of color: An empowerment perspective. *Social Work, 35*(2), 149-153.

Habermas, J. (1979). *Communication and the evolution of society.* Boston: Beacon Press.

Hall, B. L. (1981). Participatory research, popular knowledge and power. A personal reflection. *Convergence, 14*(3), 6-17.

Hall, E. T. (1966). *The hidden dimension.* Garden City, NY: Doubleday.

Hall, E. T. (1974). *Handbook for proxemic research.* Washington, DC: Society for the Anthropology of Visual Communication.

Harwood, D. (1991). Action research vs. interaction analysis: A time for reconciliation? A reply to Barry Hutchinson. *British Educational Research Journal, 17,* 67-72.

Herr, K. (1993). (Field notes). Unpublished raw data.

Herr, K., & Anderson, G. L. (1993). Oral history for student empowerment: Capturing students' inner voices. *Qualitative Studies in Education, 6*(3), 185-196.

Holland, P. (1992). Recovering the story: Understanding practice through interpretation of educational narratives. In N. Haggerson & A. Bowman (Eds.), *Informing educational policy and practice through interpretive inquiry* (pp. 199-215). Lancaster, PA: Technomic.

Holly, P. (1989). Action research: Cul-de-sac or turnpike? *Peabody Journal of Education, 64*(3), 71-100.

Holmes Group. (1990). *Tomorrow's schools: Principles for the design of professional development schools.* East Lansing, MI: The Holmes Group.

Hopkins, D. (1985). *A teacher's guide to classroom research.* London: Open University Press.

Horton, M., Bell, B., Gaventa, J., & Peters, J. M. (1990). *We make the road by walking: Conversations on education and social change.* Philadelphia: Temple University Press.

Huling, L., & Johnson, W. (1983). A strategy for helping teachers integrate research into teaching. *Teacher Educator, 19*(2), 11-18.

Hurston, Z. N. (1935). *Mules and men.* Philadelphia: J. B. Lippincott.

Hurston, Z. N. (1985). *Spunk: The selected stories.* Berkeley, CA: Turtle Island Foundation.

Hutchinson, B., & Whitehouse, P. (1986). Action research, professional competence and school organization. *British Educational Research Journal, 12*(11), 85-94.

Jackson, P. W. (1968). *Life in classrooms.* New York: Holt, Rinehart & Winston.

Janesick, V. J. (1982). Of snakes and circles: Making sense of classroom group processes through a case study. *Curriculum Inquiry, 12,* 161-185.

Janesick, V. J. (1990, April). *Proud to be deaf: An ethnographic study of deaf culture.* Paper presented at the Qualitative Research Education Conference, University of Georgia, Athens.

Kemmis, S. (Ed.). (1982). *The action research reader.* Geelong, Victoria, BC: Deaken University Press.

Kemmis, S., & McTaggart, R. (1982). *The action research planner,* Geelong Victoria, BC: Deakin University Press.

Kerlinger, F. N. (1986). *Foundation of behavior research* (3rd ed.). New York: Holt, Rinehart & Winston.

Kincheloe, J. L. (1991). *Teachers as researchers: Qualitative inquiry as a path to empowerment.* Philadelphia: Falmer Press.

Kyle, D., & Hovda, R. (1987a). The potential and practice of action research, part I. *Peabody Journal of Education, 64*(2), 80-95.

Kyle, D., & Hovda, R. (1987b). The potential and practice of action research, part II. *Peabody Journal of Education, 64*(3), 170-175.

Lanman, B., & Mehafy, G. (1988). *Oral history in the secondary school classroom.* Provo, UT: Oral History Association.

Lather, P. (1986). Research as praxis. *Harvard Educational Review, 56*(3), 257-277.

Lawn, M. A. (1989). Being caught in schoolwork: The possibilities of research in teachers' work. In W. Carr (Ed.), *Quality in teaching: Arguments for a reflective profession* (pp. 147-161). London: Falmer Press.

LeCompte, M. D. (1969). The dilemmas of inner city school reform: The Woodlawn Experimental School Project. Unpublished masters thesis. University of Chicago, IL.

LeCompte, M., & Preissle, J. (1993). *Ethnography and qualitative design in educational research* (2nd ed.). New York: Academic Press.

Lewin, K. (1946). Action research and minority problems. *Journal of Social Issues, 2*(4), 34-46.

Lewin, K. (1948). *Resolving social conflicts.* New York: Harper & Row.

Lieberman, A., & Miller, L. (1984). School improvement: Themes and variations. *Teachers College Record, 86,* 4-19.

Lindblom, C., & Cohen, D. (1979). *Usable knowledge: Social science and social problem solving.* New Haven, CT: Yale University Press.

Lincoln, Y., & Guba, E. (1985). *Naturalistic inquiry.* Beverly Hills, CA: Sage.

Liston, D. P., & Zeichner, K. M. (1991). *Teacher education and the social conditions of schooling.* New York: Routledge.

Literacies Institute (1993). *Children's voices, teachers' stories: Papers from the Brookline Teacher Researcher Seminar.* Technical Report No. 11. Newton, MA: The Literacies Institute.

Longstreet, W. (1982). Action research: a paradigm. *Educational Forum, 46*(2), 135-158.

Lubeck, S. (1985). *Sandbox society: Early education in black and white America—A comparative ethnography.* Philadelphia: Falmer Press.

Malinowski, B. (1922). *Argonauts of the western Pacific.* New York: E. P. Dutton.

Martin, N. (1987). On the move: Teacher-researchers. In D. Goswami & P. Stillman (Eds.), *Reclaiming the classroom: Teacher research as an agency for change* (pp. 20-28). Upper Montclair, NJ: Boynton/Cook.

Martinez, L. (1993). *Teacher research in the opciones para mujeres program.* Unpublished manuscript.

Maslow, A. H. (1970). *Motivation and personality.* New York: Harper & Row.

McCutcheon, G., & Jung, B. (1990). Alternative perspectives on action research. *Theory into Practice, 29*(3), 144-151.

McKernan, J. (1988). The countenance of curriculum action research: Traditional, collaborative, and emancipatory-critical conceptions. *Journal of Curriculum and Supervision, 3*(3), 173-200.

McKernan, J. (1991). *Curriculum action research: A handbook of methods and resources for the reflective practitioner.* New York: St. Martin's Press.

McLaren, P. (1989). *Life in schools: An introduction to critical pedagogy in the foundations of education.* New York: Longman.

McNeil, L. M. (1986). *Contradictions of control: School structure and school knowledge.* New York: Routledge.

McTaggart, R. (1989). Bureaucratic rationality and the self-educating profession: The problem of teacher privatism. *Journal of Curriculum Studies, 21*(4), 345-361.

Mehan, H. (1979). *Learning lessons: Social organization in the classroom.* Cambridge, MA: Harvard University Press.

Merriam, S. B. (1991). *Case study research in education: A qualitative approach.* San Francisco: Jossey-Bass.

Miller, J. (1990). *Creating spaces and finding voices: Teachers collaborating for empowerment.* Albany: State University of New York Press.

Mishler, E. G. (1986). *Research interviewing: Context and narrative.* Cambridge, MA: Harvard University Press.

Myers, M. (1985). *The teacher-researcher: How to study writing in the classroom.* Urbana, IL: National Council of Teachers of English.

Newkirk, T. (Ed.). (1992). *Workshop by and for teachers (4): The teacher as researcher.* Portsmouth, NH: Heinemann.

Nihlen, A. S. (1976). *The white working class in school: A study of first grade girls and their parents.* Unpublished doctoral dissertation, University of New Mexico.

Nihlen, A. S. (1992, April). *Views from the bottom: Homeless definitions of self.* Paper presented at the annual meeting of the American Anthropological Association, San Francisco.

Noffke, S. E. (1990, April). *Action research and the work of teachers.* Paper presented at the annual meeting of the American Educational Research Association, Boston.

Noffke, S. E. (Forthcoming). Action research and democratic schooling: Potentials and problematics. In Susan E. Noffke and Robert Stevenson, *Practically Critical: Explorations in educational action research.* New York: Teachers College Press.

Noffke, S. E., & Brennan, M. (1991). Action research and reflective student teaching at the University of Wisconsin-Madison: Issues and examples. In B. R. Tabachnik & K. Zeichner (Eds.), *Issues and practices in inquiry-oriented teacher education* (pp. 186-201). London: Falmer Press.

Noffke, S., & Stevenson, R. (Eds.). (1994). *Practically critical: Exploration in educational action research.* New York: Teachers College Press.

Oakes, J., Hare, S. E., & Sirotnik, K. A. (1986). Collaborative inquiry: A congenial paradigm in a cantankerous world. *Teachers College Record, 87,* 545-561.

Oberg, A., & McCutcheon, G. (1987). Teachers' experience doing action research. *Peabody Journal of Education, 64*(2), 116-127.

Ogbu, J. U. (1974). *The next generation: An ethnography of education in an urban neighborhood.* New York: Academic Press.

Oja, S., & Ham, M. (1984). A cognitive-developmental approach to collaborative action research with teachers. *Teachers College Record, 86,* 171-192.

Ortega, L. (1993). *Look at my teaching: Investigation of surface and hidden curriculum.* Unpublished manuscript.

Patton, M. Q. (1980). *Qualitative evaluation methods.* Beverly Hills, CA: Sage.

Pearson, J. (1993). *Whose classroom—Whose management?* Unpublished manuscript.

Polanyi, M. (1958). *Personal knowledge.* Chicago: University of Chicago Press.

Raisch, M. L. (1992). *A description and analysis of secondary student teachers and their cooperating teachers as teacher-researchers.* Unpublished doctoral dissertation, The University of New Mexico.

Reed, C., & Williams, R. C. (1993, April). *Institutionalizing action research in the Puget Sound Educational Consortium member districts.* Paper presented at the annual meeting of the American Educational Research Association, Atlanta.

Richards, M. (1989). A teacher's action research study: The "bums" of 8H (A humanistic view of motivational strategies with low achievers). *Peabody Journal of Education, 64*(2), 65-79.

Robinson, V. M. (1993). *Problem-based methodology: Research for the improvement of practice.* Oxford, UK: Pergamon.

Roman, L. (1992). The political significance of other ways of narrating ethnography: A feminist materialist approach. In M. LeCompte, W. Millroy, & J. Preissle (Eds.), *The handbook of qualitative research in education* (pp. 555-592). San Diego: Academic Press.

Rose, S. (1990). Advocacy/empowerment: An approach to clinical practice for social work. *Journal of Sociology and Social Welfare, 17,* 41-51.

Rosenholtz, S. (1989). *Teachers' workplace.* New York: Longman.

Ross, D. D. (1983, April). *Action research in a university laboratory school: An interview study.* Paper presented at the annual meeting of the American Educational Research Association, Montreal.

Ross, D. D. (1989). Action research for pre-service teachers: A description of why and how. *Peabody Journal of Education, 64*(3), 131-150.

Rowntree, D. (1981). *Statistics without tears: A primer for non-mathematicians.* New York: Penguin.

Rudduck, J. (1985). Teacher research and research-based teacher education. *Journal of Education for Teaching, 11*(3), 281-289.

Russell, R. (1992). Out of the silence: Developing teacher voice. In Gitlin et al. (Eds.), *Teachers' voices for school change* (pp. 89-117). New York: Teachers College Press.

Saavedra, E. (1994). *Teacher transformation: Creating texts and contexts in study groups.* Unpublished doctoral dissertation, The University of Arizona.

Sanders, D., & McCutcheon, G. (1986). The development of practical theories of teaching. *Journal of Curriculum and Supervision, 2*(1), 50-67.

Sanford, N. (1970). Whatever happened to action research? *Journal of Social Issues, 26,* 3-23.

Sarason, S. (1971). *The culture of the school and the problem of change.* Boston: Allyn & Bacon.

Schaefer, R. J. (1967). *The school as a center of inquiry.* New York: Harper & Row.

Schon, D. A. (1971). *Beyond the stable state.* London: Temple Smith.

Schon, D. A. (1983). *The reflective practitioner: How professionals think in action.* New York: Basic Books.

Schubert, W. H., & Schubert, A. L. (1984, April). *Sources of a theory of action research in progressive education.* Paper presented at the annual meeting of the American Educational Research Association, New Orleans.

Short, K., Connor, C., Crawford, K., Kahn, L., Kaser, S., & Sherman, P. (1993, April). *Teacher study groups: Exploring literacy issues through collaborative dialogue.* Paper presented at the annual meeting of the American Educational Research Association, Atlanta.

Smith, G. (1975). Action research: Experimental social administration? In R. Lees & G. Smith (Eds.), *Action research in community development* (pp. 77-95). London: Heinemann.

Smith, L. M., & Geoffrey, W. (1968). *The complexities of an urban classroom: An analysis toward a general theory of teaching.* New York: Holt, Rinehart & Winston.

SooHoo, S. (1991, April). *We've got rhythm, who can ask for anything more?* Paper presented at the annual meeting of the American Educational Research Association, San Francisco.

Spradley, J. (1979). *The ethnographic interview.* New York: Holt, Rinehart & Winston.

Spradley, J. (1980). *Participant observation.* New York: Holt, Rinehart & Winston.

Spindler, G. (1982). *Doing the enthnography of schooling.* New York: Holt, Rinehart & Winston.

Stake, R. (1986). An evolutionary view of educational improvement. In E. R. House (Ed.), *New directions in educational evaluation* (pp. 89-102). London: Falmer Press.

Staples, C. (1993). *Under the circumstances: A case study of a new teacher of "at-risk" students.* Unpublished doctoral dissertation, University of New Mexico.

Strommen, A. (1991). *Teacher researcher.* Unpublished manuscript.

Stubbs, M. L. (1989). *Training would-be teachers to do research: A practical account.* Wellesley College, MA: Wellesley College Center for Research on Women.

Tandon, R. (1981). Participatory research in the empowerment of people. *Convergence, 14*(3), 20-29.

Terkel, S. (1974). *Working: People talk about what they do all day and how they feel about what they do.* New York: Pantheon.

Terkel, S. (1980). *American dreams, lost and found.* New York: Ballantine.

Thorne, B. (1984, October). *Rethinking the ways we teach children.* Keynote address presented at Michigan State University.

Tikunoff, J., Ward, B., & Griffin, G. (1979). *Interactive research and development on teaching study.* San Francisco: Far West Laboratory for Educational Research and Development.

Tom, A. R. (1985). Inquiring into inquiry-oriented teacher education. *Journal of Teacher Education, 46*(5), 35-44.

Torbert, W. (1981). Why educational research has been so uneducational: The case for a new model of social science based on collaborative inquiry. In P. Reason & J. Rowan (Eds.), *Human inquiry: A sourcebook of new paradigm research* (pp. 141-151). New York: John Wiley.

Tripp, D. H. (1990). Socially critical action research. *Theory into Practice, 29*(3), 158-166.

Tuchman, G. (1994). Historical social science: Methodologies, methods, and meanings. In N. K. Denzin & Y. S. Lincoln (Eds.), *Handbook of qualitative research* (pp. 306-323). Thousand Oaks, CA: Sage.

University of New Mexico. (1991). *The oral history program brochure.* Albuquerque: University of New Mexico.

Walker, R. (1985). *Doing research: A handbook for teachers.* London: Methuen.

Walker, R., & Weidel, J. (1985). Using photographs in a discipline of words. In R. G. Burgess (Ed.), *Field methods in the study of education* (pp. 121-147). Lewes, UK: Falmer Press.

Wallat, C., Green, J. L., Conlin, S. M., & Haramis, M. (1981). Issues related to action research in the classroom: The teacher and researcher as a team. In J. L. Green & C. Wallat (Eds.), *Ethnography and language in educational settings* (pp. 87-111). Norwood, NJ: Ablex.

Watkins, K. (1991, April). *Validity in action research.* Paper presented at the annual meeting of the American Educational Research Association, Chicago.

Weiner, G. (1989). Professional self-knowledge versus social justice: A critical analysis of the teacher-researcher movement. *British Educational Research Journal, 15,* 41-51.

Whitford, B. L., Schlechty, P. C., & Shelor, L. G. (1989). Sustaining action research through collaboration: Inquiries for invention. *Peabody Journal of Education, 64*(3), 151-169.

Whyte, J. B. (1987). Issues and dilemmas in action research. In G. Wolford (Ed.), *Doing sociology of education* (pp. 28-49). Philadelphia: Falmer Press.

Winter, R. (1987). *Action research and the nature of social inquiry: Professional innovation and educational work.* Aldershot, UK: Avevury.

Witherell, C., & Noddings, N. (Eds.). (1991). *Stories lives tell: Narrative and dialogue in education.* New York: Teachers College Press.

Wolcott, H. (1973). *The man in the principal's office: An ethnography.* New York: Holt, Rinehart & Winston.

Wolcott, H. (1992). Posturing in qualitative research. In M. LeCompte, W. Millroy, & J. Preissle (Eds.), *The handbook of qualitative research in education* (pp. 3-52). New York: Academic Press.

Wood, P. (1988). Action research: A field perspective. *Journal of Education for Teaching, 14*(2), 135-150.

Yin, R. K. (1989). *Case study research: Design and methods.* Newbury Park, CA: Sage.

Yopo, B. (1984). *Metodologia de la investigacion participativa.* Patzcuaro, Michoacan, Mexico: CREFAL.

Zacanella, D. (1993). Personal communication with the authors.

Zeichner, K. (1981). Reflective teaching and field based experience in teacher education. *Interchange, 12*(4), 1-22.

Index

Action research, xxi, 1-2, 11-14, 63,
    99
  collaborative, 43
  contrasted with participatory
    research, 17
  cooperative, 13
  critical, 16
  feminist, 15
  spiral, 12, 16, 31, 55, 70, 79, 114,
    120, 127, 156-57, 169
  transformative, 30
Action science, 18-19
Advocacy, 42
Altrichter, H., 180
Analysis:
  analytic induction, 166-167
  constant comparison, 167
  construction, 110
  discourse, 161

  ethnographic, 163
  final, 156-157
  ongoing, 155-156
  reflection, 155-156
  Spradley, 163-166
Anderson, G. L., 39, 80, 105, 180
Anthropology, 131
  anthropologists, 111, 121, 131,
    147, 148
Archives and documents, 151-153
Argyris, C., 5, 12, 18-19, 23, 25, 105
Assumptive modes, 108-112, 114
Audiotaping, 50, 66, 94, 99, 117,
    179-180

Ballenger, C., 48, 66-70, 175
Biklen, S., 158-160
Bogdan, R., 158-160

Boston Women's Teachers' Group, 20
Bruner, J., 35

C.A.R.E. *See* Center for Applied Research in Education
Case study research, 10, 20, 170
Center for Applied Research in Education (C.A.R.E), 19
Chandler, S., 28
Chism, N., 46
Clandinin, J., 31-33, 122-123
Cobb, K., 126-127
Cochran-Smith, M., 24, 40, 107-108, 111-112, 180
Coding, 157-158
  activity, 159
  context, 158
  event, 159
  methods, 160
  participant ways of thinking, 159
  perspective, 159
  process, 159
  relationship and social structure, 160
  setting, 158
  situation, 158
  strategy, 160
Collaboration, 2, 7, 16, 20, 22, 28, 32, 38, 61, 85, 95
Connelly, M., 31-33, 122-123
Consent form, 116-117
Constructive, 112, 114
Corey, 13, 23
Counts, G., 42
"Critical" friend, 4, 32, 48, 64, 114, 181
Critical theory, 18
Culture, 119
Cunningham, J., 30
Curriculum:
  shadow, 66-67
  teacher's, 67

Delpit, L., 43
de Schutter, A., 17
Deskilling, 5, 20
Dewey, J., 11, 18, 23, 33-34
Diaries, 108, 153-155
Dicker, M., 176-177, 179-180, 181
Discourse analysis, 161
  constraints, 161-162
  content, 162
  dilemma, 161
  document, 162
  episode, 163
  sociometric, 163
Duckworth, E., 182
Dynamic conservatism, 25, 38

Educative Research Project, 56
Educators' Forum, 48, 77-79, 181
Elliott, J., 14, 23, 150
Emancipatory research. *See* Participatory research
Emerson Elementary School Oral History Project, 119, 121, 153
Emic, 111, 119, 167
Epistemology, 27-36
Etic, 111
Ethnography, 4, 20, 119, 131, 168-169
  analysis, 163
  componential, 166
  domain, 163-164
  taxonomic, 164-166
  constitutive, 167
  educational, 168-169
  interview, 118-120
  microethnography, 148
Evans, C., 48, 77-79, 114, 181

Feminist researchers, 15, 28, 71, 112, 121
Field notes, 97-98
Freire, P., 16-17, 20, 23

Garcia, G., 136-138
Gaventa, J., 16
Generative themes, 16
Gitlin, A., 22, 40-41, 56
Glaser, B., 120, 167
Green, J., 28-29
Greene, J., 30, 44
Grounded theory, 120
Guba, E., 27, 33, 157, 167

Hall, E., 141-143
Herr, K., 80, 174-175, 177-178, 180
Highlander Center, 16
Historical sources. *See* Archives
    and documents
Holland, P., 35
Holly, P., 38-39, 100
Holmes Group, 22, 41, 119
Holtz, A., 70-77
Horizontal Evaluation, 57-58
Horton, M., 16
Hutchinson, B., 39-40

Ideology, 24
Indexing interviews, 118
Inquiry, 107
"Insider" research, 2, 4, 27, 29, 133
Interviews, 82-85, 115-118
    checklists, 128
    contrast, 119-120
    descriptive, 119
    disadvantages of, 115
    ethnographic, 82, 118-120
    inventories, 128
    narrative, 20, 31, 121-122
    oral history, 121-122
    questionnaires, 50 124-128
    rating scales, 128
    structured, 123-124

Journals, 48, 50, 62, 108, 64, 66, 70-
    77, 153-155, 179

Kemmis, S., 3, 15-16, 23, 138
Kincheloe, J., 24, 106
Knowledge, xvi
    creation, xvi, 6,
    dissemination, xvi
    expert, xvi
    local, 4
    personal, 34
    politics of, 36
    subjugated, 37, 42
    tacit, 4, 65, 70, 79, 80
    utilization, xvi
    valid, 41-42
Knowledge base, xviii

Lather, P., 23-24, 31
Lawn, M., 173
LeCompte, M., 108-111, 148, 157,
    167
Lewin, K., 11-12, 18, 23
Lincoln, Y., 27, 33, 157, 167
Literacy, 66-70
Local knowledge, 112
Lytle, S., 24, 40, 107-108, 111-112,
    180

Making the familiar strange, 115,
    165, 169
Mansdoerfer, S., xv
Mapping, 141-147
Martin, N., 171
Martinez, L., 125, 128
McCutcheon, G., 3, 19, 47
McKernan, J., 3, 10-11, 139, 147-
    148, 150, 153-154, 161, 163
McTaggart, R., 3, 21, 138
Mehan, H., 167-168
Merriam, S., 170

Micropolitics, 37
Miller, J., 25-26, 155
Minority researchers, 112, 121
Mishler, E., 35
Multiple methods, 168

Narratives. *See* Interviews
Naturalistic generalization, 33-34,
    104
Naturalistic research.
    See Qualitative research
Nihlen, A., 112, 119, 131, 160-161
Noffke, S., ix-xi, 21, 24

Objectivity, 110-111, 130
Observation, 129-130
    checklists, 138, 139
    mapping, 141-147
    material cultural inventories,
        147-148
    participant observation, 130-138
    personal action logs, 138
    photography, still, 148, 151
    rating scales, 138, 139
    video, 148-151
    visual recordings, 148-151
Oral history, 121-122, 169
Organizational learning, 18
Ortega, L., 150-151

Paradigms:
    humanities, 180
    modernist, xx
    naturalist, xx
    positivist, xx, 20, 27
Participatory research, 16-18
Pearson, J., 134-136, 145-146, 172
Peterson, B., 42
Politics of practitioner research, 36-
    44
Posch, P., 180

Preissle, J., 108-111, 157, 167
Professionalism, 20-21, 36, 39-42
Proxemics, 141, 143

Qualitative research, xx-xxi, 5, 20,
    106-170, 178
Quantitative research, 5, 15, 20, 106
Questionnaires. *See* Interviews

Racism, 75-76, 85-94, 100-103
Raisch, M., 22, 154
Reactivity, 111
Reflection, xxi, 2, 11, 42, 51, 55
    in action, 180
    on action, xxi
    process, 2
Rethinking Schools, 42
Richards, M., 32, 47-48, 51-55, 174,
    177
Robinson, V., 19, 104-105
Roman, L., 28
Russell, R., 47, 55-60, 114, 181

Sanders, D., 46
Schon, D., 5, 11-12, 18, 20, 24-25,
    38-39, 41, 100, 180
Shadowing, 48, 50, 61
Silencing, 55-58, 105
Social engineering, xxi, 15, 42
Soohoo, S., 22, 47-48, 61-66
Spradley, J., 119-120, 131-132, 134,
    163-166
Stake, R., 33-35
Staples, C., 143, 144, 147
Stenhouse, L., 14, 23
Strauss, A., 120, 167
Strommen, A., 113-114
Stubbs, M., 47, 77-79, 114, 181
Study groups, 7, 25, 32, 59, 70-71
Subjectivity, 110-111, 114, 121, 133
    systematic subjectivity, 108

Tape recorder, 117-118
Teacher:
    isolation, 70
    research, 1, 21,
    teachers-as-researchers
        movement, 14
Tenorio, R., 42
Theory development, 66-70
Time, lack of, 59
Transcription, 118
Transferability, 33
Triangulation, 31, 114, 156, 168
Trustworthiness, 27

Validity, 27-33
    catalytic, 30, 104
    democratic, 30, 104
    dialogic, 32, 104
    external, 27, 104
    internal, 27, 104
    local, 30

outcome, 30, 104
process, 31, 104
Vasquez, C., 121
Vicarious experience, 34
Video cam, 148-151
Voice, 55-56, 60-65, 79, 84, 87, 96,
    102, 105

Walker, R., 151
Watkins, K., 31
Whitehouse, P., 39-40
Winter, R., 23
Wolcott, H., 107, 169

Yopo, B., 17

Zeichner, K., 21
Ziegler, A., 122
Zitlow, C., 46